Thy Queendom Come

Viv Love

Printed in the United States of America.
ISBN: 978-0-9982706-3-0
First Printing, 2019
Val Pugh Publishing
www.valpughlove.com
Shreveport, LA 71109

This book is dedicated to

my supporters.

"Feels so good being bad
There's no way I'm turning back
Now the pain is for pleasure
'Cause nothing can measure."

Rihanna

1

Vivian

He raped me, and I want revenge.
Those were the first words I saw in the
subject line when I opened my email this
morning. I quickly placed my cup of coffee
on my desk and directed my focus to that
email. When I opened it, a picture of a young
woman with bruises all over her body greeted
me. Her face was swollen and covered in
blood. Her eyes were black with a bloodshot
in the left eye. Pain and anger instantly filled
my heart. As I scrolled through the email, I
saw several more pictures of her scars from
the horrible ordeal. Her legs were bruised
with fingerprints from where her attacker had
forced her legs open. Another image showed
her bloody finger where her nail broke during
her attempt to fight off the monster that

violated her. I spared myself the heartache of viewing the remaining pictures. Instead, I scrolled back up to the top of the email and continued to read her text.

"I had been working with the deacon board at my church to prepare for an upcoming event. Most times, other members would be in the church doing different things for their committees. This night, I was alone with Deacon Rogers. At first, all was well. We discussed the plans for the event, and we shared great ideas on making it a success. While we talked, I noticed how he'd stare at me, but I shook it off as paranoia and continued the discussion. Finally, after we covered everything, I prepared to leave.

"As I gathered my belongings, Deacon Rogers went to the door and slowly closed it. I asked him what he was doing, and he told me that we had some unfinished business. I laughed a nervous laugh and proceeded to walk towards the door. I told him that I thought we had covered enough for the night and we could meet again soon. That's when he grabbed me and aggressively pulled me close to him. He attempted to kiss my lips, but I turned my head and asked him to stop. We continued to struggle, and I

fought him off for a while. However, the more I rejected him, the stronger he became. It was as if the rejection fueled his rage. I eventually grew tired of fighting as my mind drifted to a faraway place.

"After what seemed like an hour or more, he stopped and began to re-dress himself. I laid in my blood for a few minutes as I gathered my thoughts and prayed that I would awaken from that nightmare. His raspy voice interrupted my thoughts with threats of ruining my existence and even killing me if I breathed a word of the rape to anyone. As I cried silently, he quickly exited the office and left the church without even glancing back at me. I contemplated calling the police, but I knew that would be a bad look for the church. I don't even think anyone would believe that their precious Deacon Rogers would do such a thing.

"I thought about killing myself right there on the floor of his office, but that wouldn't stop him from hurting another woman. Then, I remembered hearing about your services, and I gained enough strength to get myself together. I went home and cleaned up the mess that he made of my body, and now I'm ready for revenge. I don't care

how much it costs; I just want him to pay for what he did to me. Please help me."

Her words weighed on me heavily as I sat back in my chair and stared at the sun through the clouds. How could the same Creator of something so beautiful allow monsters like Deacon Rogers to roam the earth and hurt women? I tried to think of a response to her email, but nothing came to me. For the first time in a long time, I had no immediate idea of seeking revenge. Usually, my clients were only victims of bad marriages with cheating, lying, or even abusive husbands. I dealt with an occasional rape victim, but the attacker was typically the woman's husband who was fed up with his wife not having sex with him. He never intended to hurt his wife; he just wanted to have sex with her. While rape is rape and no is no, we didn't count that as an actual attack. However, this was indeed a rape case. It was the epitome of sexual violation.

Although I couldn't immediately think of a way to avenge her issue, I knew that I needed to respond to her so that she wouldn't feel more alone than she already felt. I pressed the reply button, and simply typed: *I will call you soon. He will pay.* Then,

I sat back in my chair and waited for Maria to buzz me to let me know that Tosha had arrived. The details in the email left me so emotionally drained that I decided to call my mother. She is a rape survivor, and she has spoken to so many women over the years about regaining their power after all hope is gone. Queen and I have our methods of getting revenge, and they usually work. This time, though, I believe my client will need some emotional healing first.

I picked up the handset and began to dial my mother's number slowly. We hadn't spoken in months because she doesn't agree with the services that I provide to my clients. She found out about Queen after I attended one of her seminars. At the event, a lady spoke about her story and how she had been raped multiple times throughout her life by her cousin. She told her mother about it, but her mom simply swept it under the rug. She went on to say that the cousin had molested so many relatives, and the family continued to ignore it. She finally decided to move to a new city to start a fresh life. It had been years since she went home. She lived with resentment towards her elders for not being there when she needed them. She felt angry because no one protected her from the repeated violations of her body, mind, and character.

While the lady spoke, I felt myself become more and more enraged. I thought about how Frankie C. had hurt my mother when I was a newborn. I felt jealous of my mother because she got the pleasure of killing him. I thought about all the times my clients came to me and spoke of how their husbands forced them to have sex when they didn't want to do it. As I continued to listen to the woman speak, I knew that I needed to help her. Once the seminar ended, I pushed my way through the crowd of over two hundred women until I reached the woman that had captured my full attention. I walked her over to a secluded area and expressed my condolences about her story. Then, I proceeded to tell her about my services.

As I spoke to her, I knew that I had gained her interest. Just as I was reaching into my purse to give her a card, my mother cleared her throat and asked what I was doing. Bella's presence scared the young lady away, and I was unable to save her. I have regretted that moment every second since we spoke, and I vowed to save the next woman that shared her pain. Bella and I had a heated argument and said some horrible things to each other. I know that neither of us meant those things, but we were both too stubborn to call each other first. However, the email that I received this morning wouldn't allow me to be stubborn any longer. I dialed my mother's number and let it ring until her voicemail picked up. In my mind, she purposely ignored my call because she was still salty about our fight. However, I shook that thought away and left a message anyway.

"Hi, Ma… It's me. Listen, I know things ended badly the last time we spoke. I'm sorry for the awful things I said to you. I hope you can forgive me. I need you, Ma. I have a client that needs both of us. Someone raped her. Please help me help her. I hope to hear from you soon. I love you."

I pressed the end button and laid my head back on the headrest of my leather chair. I knew I'd have to dig deep into my counseling side with this case. Hopefully, Bella can help me ensure that this girl is strong enough to function. I don't want to introduce her to the dark side so soon. Queen's revenge will have to wait.

2

Tosha

It's been about two months since Tyrone and I separated. After the ordeal at the queendom, we tried traditional marriage counseling. However, he couldn't seem to get over the fact that I allowed his two bitches to stick piping hot dildos up his ass. Lucky for him, I loved him too much to let the torture continue. Although I was the one who contacted Vivian McQueen for help with getting revenge on my cheating husband, I still couldn't bring myself to watch those women inflict so much pain and humiliation on Tyrone. I was just fed up with years of infidelity and mental abuse that I dealt with in my marriage. I needed him to feel the pain that ran so deeply through my heart. However, I loved him more than I loved myself. So, I couldn't allow them to continue to hurt him.

Since then, Vivian has been asking me to work part-time with Queen. She saw a dark side of me that even I didn't know existed. She initially said she wanted to become more deeply involved with me. Everything about that sounded sexual, so I've been skeptical about even meeting with her to discuss her thoughts. Still, my curiosity has been getting the best of me, so I finally agreed to meet her. I had also been avoiding her calls and emails because I think my husband's two bitches have been working with her. I still stalk them occasionally when I fly to Shreveport, and I know I saw her car at their shop one day.

***

When I parked my car in front of McQueen Towers, my heart began to race. My thoughts became clouded with scenes from the night we tortured Tyrone at the Queendom. I thought about the physical pain he endured, and I wondered if he deserved that level of torture. Then, my mind flashed to the many times he embarrassed me with his infidelity. I thought about the times I heard the neighbors whispering as I passed by or the times I caught him creeping out of his bitch's backyard. My pain for him was replaced with anger, and I suddenly found the energy to get out my car and head to my meeting with Vivian.

I pushed the elevator button and waited for it to come down so I could go up to her office. As I stood there, I looked around and admired how elegantly she had the area decorated. There was a beautiful fountain with neon lights in the center of the floor. Each corner contained an oversized palm tree in a ceramic pot adorned with hand-painted African images. I looked around the area as I continued to admire the décor, and I noticed that I was not alone. I was startled by a person staring at me at the far end of the long hallway.

At first glance, it appeared that they were looking out the window. However, when I stared more closely, I realized the person was looking directly at me. I pushed the elevator button again because it was taking an unusually long time to come down.

It finally opened as the person began to walk quickly towards me. An eerie feeling came over me as I immediately stepped into the elevator and pressed the button to close the door before they made it down the hall. The emotional rollercoaster that I've been on for the past few months could have me tripping, but something didn't feel right about what had just happened. I decided to shake it off as I entered Vivian's office.

"Greetings Mrs. Blackshire. Vivian is expecting you. I'll let her know you're on your way back," Maria said as she picked up the vintage handset and buzzed Vivian's office.

When I entered the room, Vivian was sitting at her desk thumbing through some paperwork. She had a look on her face that I'd never seen before. For the first time, she seemed to be human with emotions.

"I hope I'm not interrupting anything," I said to break the silence.

"Oh no. Everything is fine. Come on in and have a seat. How are you?" Vivian asked as she stood up and leaned across the desk to give me a peck on both cheeks.

"I'm well. I'm just trying to get my life back on track after Tyrone. We've been separated for a couple of months. We tried to work things out after his session at the Queendom, but he couldn't bring himself to forgive me. I asked if he wanted a divorce, and he said he just needed a little time to reevaluate everything."

"Yeah, you ladies did give it to him good that night. That's actually why I wanted to see you. Why have you been avoiding my calls?" Vivian asked.

"I wasn't avoiding you per se. I was just trying to work on my marriage. I needed to clear my head. I wasn't as ready for revenge as I thought I was."

"You chose that method of *healing*. You can't blame me because you and your husband's bitches caused him to get stitches in his asshole."

"*Healing... revenge* or whatever you want to call it. I'm not blaming you. I'm only saying that I spent the months following that night feeling regret and guilt. That's all," I said as I dropped my head to break her stare.

"Well, I've been trying to reach you to offer you a job."

"A job? Where? At the Queendom? Nah, I think I'll pass…"

"I'm sure you'll appreciate the ten thousand dollars signing bonus. And, it's not at the Queendom… all the time. You'll be working out of this office building the majority of the time. If there are any issues or big events, then you would be asked to attend them at the Queendom. If you feel that you can't handle the tasks before you, I will reinforce our policies."

While Vivian explained the basis of my employment with her agency, she took a step closer as she spoke each word. By the time she started talking about reinforcing policies, she was straddled across my lap with her perky breasts in my face. My suspicions were finally confirmed – this bitch is a lesbian.

"Um, Vivian… What are you doing?"

"I'm reinforcing the job offer. Does this make you nervous?" Vivian asked as she began to grind slowly and sensually in my lap while nibbling my ear lobe.

Before I could say a word, she began to kiss me. The kiss was one that I had never experienced before. It was as if her tongue was etching a magical message in my mouth. I covered my ears as the sound of her kisses got louder and louder. Finally, I woke up to my panties drenched from the dream. I reached over and turned off the alarm clock that saved me from whatever was about to happen next. Then, I sat in my bed feeling weird and embarrassed about the wetness. I thought about the strange man that was walking towards me before I got on the elevator. I wondered who he could have been. I tried not to think about the way Vivian straddled my lap and kissed me. Were those my subconscious desires or was it just a dream? Maybe the nervousness of meeting her had me going crazy. Either way, I got out of bed, took a hot shower, and tried to clear my thoughts before seeing her.

3

Cheyenne

It's been a week since that sick motherfucker raped me. I've tried my best to get back to normal, but that's been hard as hell considering how he bruised my body and gave me Chlamydia. I've cried day and night since it happened. I haven't eaten, nor have I been to the shop. Marissa, my business partner turned best friend, has been calling nonstop. I finally answered and told her that I've been sick and contagious. I knew she'd stop trying to be my savior once she heard that. That also gave me more alone time to think about whether I should kill that dirty ass deacon. The night it happened, I immediately reached out to Vivian McQueen. I know she'll know how to handle this without me being convicted of any crimes. I expected an immediate response from her. However, she sent back a simple message with no instructions. I thought that was strange because she's usually quick on her feet. That sharpness came from our mother.

Before you start flipping back to see if you missed something, here's my story. My name is Cheyenne Johnson, but I was born Charles Bourdeaux. I'm Vivian's older brother. We have the same mother, but we grew up in separate homes. My father raised our brother and me, and our mother raised Vivian. I always knew I was different, but I was too afraid to tell my father because he was hella gangster and took no shit from anyone. Many nights, I longed to call my mother for comfort. However, I never knew where to begin. I grew up needing her, wanting her, and wondering why she never came back for us. I always had her number, but I couldn't bring myself to dial the last digit. For years, I would hang up before I finished dialing.

I resented her for a long time because she left us with our horrible ass father. He gave her hell, so I don't know why she expected him to treat us any better. Vincent always knew I had sway in my walk and sass in my talk. So he often called me a faggot, sissy, fagitron, and any other demeaning names he could think of when he was angry. I often wished I could grow up to be stronger and much bigger than he was so I could kick his ass when he tried to tear me down again. My brother, on the other hand, was a tough guy who had all the girls and loved the street life like our father. Vinny loved him and despised me so much. A few of the guys on his payroll used to flirt with me whenever my father wasn't around. I always felt like they were setting me up, so I never gave in to their advances. I just tried my best to act straight until I could leave my father's house.

I came across Vivian by chance, and my sister is something else. That heffa is a major boss, and she's paid like a mofo. She owns a counseling agency that teaches women empowerment through her dominatrix queendom. I've actually been there before. Long story short, Marissa and I accidentally dated the same guy. She met him at the shop, and I met him online. I tried online dating for a split second because I hadn't been having any luck with romance. Anyway, the guy changed his name online. So, Marissa and I talked freely about our men and had no idea that we were both dating the same guy.

Oh, and his ass was married. He didn't know we knew each other until he showed up at Marissa's house and I answered the door. We were all in shock. I had to stop my girl from killing him. Somehow the wife found out about us. She contacted Viv, and Viv arranged the meeting at the Queendom. She invited us because he hurt us, but his wife controlled the session. Honey, the shit I saw in there that night sent me running to the church house. When I tell you his wife tore him a new asshole, I mean that literally.

I didn't recognize my sister at first, and they never called her by name. They call her Queen or Madam at the Queendom. When I first saw Vivian, she was wearing a mask, but her eyes were so familiar. Her voice was different, but I knew it was my sister. I wanted to wrap my arms around her, but that diva was in beast mode, and I didn't want any shit out of her. Plus, I was too ashamed to reveal my true identity in front of Marissa. She doesn't know that I wasn't born a female. We have been friends for several years. I've contemplated telling her so many times, but I just don't want things to change between us. People always start acting differently with me when they find out I'm transgender. I've spoken with Vivian on the phone over the years, but we never got around to meeting each other for lunch. I needed more time to become more comfortable with my new life.

During the time I spent getting to know myself better, I became active in my church. That's how I met Deacon Rogers. From the moment I met him, he always looked at me in a way that made me feel uncomfortable. He would even do it when his wife was around. I know she saw the looks and could sense the tension, but she never said anything. She has always been polite to me. After a while, the gawking began to fade, and I became more comfortable around him. I even went to a gathering at their home a time or two. He hardly looked my way, and I almost started to think I had just imagined things in the beginning. However, my suspicions were confirmed the night he raped me.

He mentioned that he knew my secret, and that thought stuck with me until I put two and two together. I thought back to when I first saw him at the church. He looked slightly familiar to me then. However, since I don't frequent places where older people hang out, I assumed it could have been déjà vu or something. After the horrible ordeal, I replayed our interactions over and over again until his face suddenly popped up in my childhood memories. He does business with my father. I remember seeing him at our house one day. I had just gotten home, and he was there. When our father would have company, we weren't allowed to sit around them. Therefore, I dropped my head and went straight to my bedroom the day Deacon Rogers was there. As I walked past him, he stuck his foot out. I stumbled but quickly apologized and went straight to my room.

I still can't figure out how he knows who I am though. I'm a completely different person from who he saw that day. I've had a complete sex change, and my life as Cheyenne has been so much better than my childhood. Still, a part of me wants to contact my father to tell him what happened to me, but I can't take the verbal abuse that I usually get when we speak. I just need answers. I need to understand how his friend knows the new me, and why he felt it was okay to rape me. Maybe Vivian can help me talk to him.

4

Tosha

I leerily entered McQueen Towers and gave the lobby a quick scan. Unlike in my dream the night before, the area was busy. Even better, there wasn't a strange person walking quickly toward me. I took the elevator to Vivian's office. On the ride up to the penthouse suite, I calmed my rapidly beating heart and quick breaths before opening the Victorian-style office door that led to the waiting area that Maria occupies. As I exited the elevator, I heard faint laughter through the sounds of jazz music playing on the other side of the door. That put me at ease as I grabbed the crystal doorknob and entered the suite. Maria was standing in the hallway talking to someone. She didn't hear me come in, so I closed the door with a bit of force to get her attention.

"Mrs. Blackshire! Hi! You startled me. I was too busy running my mouth that I didn't even hear you come in. How have you been?"

"Hey there! I've been well. I had to find time to break away from work so I could finally come to town to meet with Vivian. Is she in?"

"Of course. You know Viv wouldn't dare miss the opportunity to see you. You must have made a mark on her because she's been talking about you all morning. I'll let her know you're here. Help yourself to some coffee, tea, or wine while you wait."

Maria's words caused butterflies to form in my stomach, so I took her up on the wine offer. I poured myself a glass of Sangiovese and peered out the window. My thoughts drifted back to last night's dream as Kenny G's *Songbird* hummed through the speakers. My kitty moistened as I imagined Vivian's soft lips on mine. I thought about the way she whispered in my ear during our first meeting and how pleasantly awkward that made me feel. As I heard footsteps approaching, I came to terms that I was prepared for whatever Vivian had in store for me.

"Good morning, Tosha. I thought you wouldn't show," Vivian's sultry voice said as

I turned around and enjoyed the seductive scent of her perfume.

"It's funny that you say so because I also thought I wouldn't show," I laughed nervously.

"What changed your mind?"

"A dream," I replied with a sly smile.

"A dream? I see. Follow me to my office so we can speak privately."

Vivian's soft fingertips grazed my face as she passed by me and headed to her office.

"Maria, hold all my calls. I need to give Tosha my undivided attention."

I followed her down the long hallway that leads to her office. She'd redecorated since the last time I was there. I noticed a painting that I hadn't seen before. It was displayed on a decorative easel beside the door to her office. The artwork was an image of her sitting on a throne chair wearing a golden bra and panties bedazzled in jewels. A lioness and cheetah lay on each side of her as if they were her protectors. Her mouth wore a slight smile while her eyes seductively stared at anyone that viewed the painting.

"I can give you the contact information for the artist who painted that picture if you'd like."

"That won't be necessary. I was just admiring how he or she captured you so well," I said slightly embarrassed that she knew I was gawking at the painting, although her back was to me.

"*He* did a great job indeed. He's one of the good ones who has never had to go to the Queendom. Unfortunately, my dark side won't allow me to let him in my life completely. But, enough about me. How have you been?"

Just when I thought I could learn a smidgen about Vivian, she changed the subject and became a closed book again. I wanted to pry, but I figured I'd play the game with her until I could warm her up – as if that was even possible.

"I've been well. Tyrone and I still live separately. I was lonely at first and wanted him to come back so we could work things out. However, he wasn't ready to forgive me yet. Go figure. So, I gave him his space and didn't push the issue. Since then, I've learned to be alone, and I've enjoyed getting to know myself better. I can't say I haven't missed him, but I have truly enjoyed my peace of mind. How have you been?" I asked trying to switch the conversation from me.

"I've been well. It's business as usual at the Queendom, and the clients continue to flow daily. Life is good. Have you considered my offer?"

"I have, but I need to know what the job entails. I mean, I know I appeared to be comfortable when we were torturing my husband, but that's not something that I could get into every day. Besides, I still live in Chicago. And, it'll be hard for me to travel so much now that I've started the catering business back home."

"I wouldn't expect you to engage in those activities daily. I just need you to be me when I'm not around. I'd give you notice of my absence in advance. I'll also cover your traveling expenses. Have you ever considered relocating? You could have a whole floor to yourself at the Queendom. That would also give me the chance to see your beautiful face more often."

Our eyes locked in a seductive stare-down as soon as she complimented me. I wondered if my dream would come true. Not that I wanted it to, but I couldn't help but wonder if I had foreseen what would happen between us. I tried to break the trance by glancing at my phone. However, she continued to look at me until I became nervous. I was finally able to break the silence.

"Is everything okay? Why are you staring at me that way?"

"Everything is fine. I just love to watch you squirm and fidget when you're near me. I turn you on, and you're afraid of how much you're attracted to me. You are the only client I have that acts so nervous around me," she said as she picked up her teacup and took a sip without breaking her stare.

"Ha… Who says I'm attracted to you? I'm simply listening to your response to my question. Of course, I did get nervous when you started staring at me mid-conversation. But, who does that? I was waiting for you to finish speaking, but that never happened," I said feeling slightly annoyed because she was right as usual.

"I enjoy watching you, Tosha. There's something magnetic about you. You have what it takes to work closely with me.

You just have to relax and trust me to train you well."

"That's the thing, Vivian. How can I trust you when I hardly even know you? All I know is bits of what you do. I don't know if you have any family or friends. I don't even know if you've ever been in a relationship before or if you're just living out some weird fantasies through my problems. I need to know more about you if I'm going to consider working with you. Tell me something."

"What do you want to know?" Vivian calmly asked.

Startled by her instant response, I cleared my throat to avoid stumbling as I spoke.

"Ahem… Um… Well… Have you ever been married?"

"No. I came close, but it was called off weeks before the wedding. What else do you want to know?"

"What made you call it off?"

"I never said *I* called it off."

"Wow. I wouldn't expect anyone to leave a woman of power like you. You're beautiful, smart, strong, and enticing. Anyone should feel honored to marry you."

"While those characteristics sound great spoken aloud, they're the very reasons he didn't want to marry me. He told me I was too strong, and he didn't think I'd be a submissive wife. He said I was too beautiful, and that would cause problems for him with other people being easily attracted to me. He felt like I was too smart, and I would make him look bad in front of his associates and friends if I knew more than he did. Of course, with me being so enticing, he would constantly worry if I'm somewhere seducing a random person. So, to save himself the embarrassment of having a smart, beautiful, strong, enticing wife, he called off the wedding," Vivian said before taking another sip from her teacup.

"So, is that what made you decide to offer your services to women like me?"

"That's part of the reason."

"What's the other part?" I asked, wondering what other heartbreaks she could have encountered.

"We'll talk more about that at a later time. I've already given you far too much personal information. That's totally against my rules of engagement. Now, I must regain control of this situation. Stand up," she said as she pushed her chair back and stood up from her desk.

"Stand up? Stand up for what? What are you about to do?" I asked as she walked to the door and engaged the lock.

"Stand up and find out."

As my heart began to pound even harder than it was pounding before I entered the elevator, I stood up and attempted to face her, but her words quickly made me turn back around.

"Did I tell you to look at me!?"

"Vivian..."

"Excuse me? What did you just call me?" she asked as she grabbed me by the waist and snatched my skirt down to the floor.

"What are you doing?" I asked refusing to say any form of a name for fear that I'd say the wrong thing.

"I'm checking to see if you're wearing a wire. The less you say, the quicker this will be. Place your hands on my desk and spread your legs."

Without a word, I did as I was told. She began to rub her hands on my hips, up and down my legs, and between my thighs. Her movements were slow and sensual. Each time she neared my vagina, it began to throb and moisten even more. However, she never touched me there. She began to move her hands up my sides and around to my breasts. She slowly turned me around and stared into my eyes as she unbuttoned my shirt. She never spoke a word. Neither did I. I just let her undress me. Once my blouse was half-way unbuttoned, she snatched the remaining buttons apart. I could hear them hit the hardwood floors beneath our feet. She removed my shirt and let it fall to the floor. I stood facing her in just my black lace panties and matching bra. She remained silent as she ran her fingers along the edge of my bra and then across my erect nipples that could almost pierce the lace that covered them. Finally, her erotic voice broke the silence.

"It seems that I was mistaken. Based on your line of questioning, I assumed you were an undercover spy either for the Feds or for the competition. That's why I was checking to see if you were wearing a wire. Forgive me. You may redress. There's a fresh shirt in the closet," she whispered in my ear.

Before she stepped away, she turned her face so that our noses barely touched. Then, she took her hand, lifted my chin, and kissed me like I'd never been kissed before. I didn't resist. I didn't turn my head or stop her. Instead, I kissed her back. Vigorously. It felt better than the kiss from the dream. I even pulled her closer to me. She seemed shocked. Still, I continued as if I didn't feel her slightly tense up. I had her. She didn't have me. I abruptly stopped kissing her, and then I grabbed my clothes from the floor near my feet. It was just the beginning of fulfilling my fantasy of her. I didn't say a word as I got dressed and prepared to exit her office. This time, she would be the one wondering what I had in mind. This time, I was in control.

5

Cheyenne

I was finally able to catch up on some rest over the weekend. I locked myself inside my house and binge-watched episodes of my favorite shows. I didn't bother to check my email or even respond to text messages or phone calls. I just needed to be alone to think of how I planned to handle Deacon Rogers' rapist ass. Although I was anxious to hear back from Vivian to hear her thoughts, I was too nervous to check my email to see if she had replied by now. Indeed, I wanted revenge. However, I wasn't mentally prepared for the backlash that I'd receive once the church found out what that devil had done to me.

Nevertheless, my curiosity was getting the best of me. Therefore, I grabbed my laptop and logged into my email. As expected, Vivian had sent me an email a few days ago. I nervously moved the cursor to the email and double-clicked it. Like her initial response after I contacted her for services, her message was to the point. It read: "Let's meet. McQueen Towers. Friday 10:00 a.m. My address is listed below. Don't be late."

My emotions became a mixture of excitement and nervousness as I looked at the calendar on my phone to check the date. I didn't realize it was already Thursday. I had been inside for practically a week without having any contact with the outside world besides the delivery guys. I hadn't even looked at myself in the mirror nor had I had anything close to a shower. Reruns, take-out, and naps kept me company while I tried to rid my thoughts of the constant reminders of the rape.

I decided to pry myself from the cozy corner of my sectional and clean up my mess of Chinese food containers, pizza boxes, water bottles, and empty potato chip bags. As I gathered the trash from my Cherrywood coffee table, my reflection began to appear in the glass in the center of the table. Seeing myself looking so disheveled fueled my anger again. How could I let that monster have so much control over me? At this point, I didn't care who found out that I wasn't born a female. I didn't care if the whole church knew and excommunicated me. I just needed revenge on that sick son of a bitch. I made up in my mind that I would walk right into Vivian's office and let her know I want that motherfucker to feel my pain multiplied.

By the time I finished cleaning up my mess and brainstorming my plan, it was almost midnight. I took a long hot shower and climbed into my king-sized sleigh bed with my laptop. Once I was settled amid the big fluffy pillows with my bonnet secured on my head, I replied to Vivian's email to let her know I would be at the meeting tomorrow. Then, I scrolled through my inbox to see if I had missed any other important messages. I had mostly received coupons, e-bills, and junk mail. I deleted the junk mail, set reminders in my calendar for the bills, and sorted my coupons in the respective folders in my inbox. As I continued to scroll through, I came across a message from an Unknown Sender. That was strange because those types of messages usually go into my Spam folder. I was more interested in reading it because the subject line read: YOUR SECRET IS NOW "OUR" SECRET. I opened the email without thinking it could be a virus because that was similar to the shit Deacon Rogers said before he raped me.

When I opened the email, I saw several pictures of me at various stages of my life. They ranged from me as a toddler to me right before I switched genders to just after my operation. I instantly knew who the Unknown Sender was, but I was baffled at how he was able to obtain so many images of me. How long had he been plotting against me? What did he even want from me? Who could he be working with behind the scenes? A million questions flooded my mind. What had I done to deserve such torture and pain?

I grew up somewhat a loner. I kept to myself and tried to stay out of trouble. I had childhood friends who accepted me as I was, but I never really connected with any one person in particular. I always felt different from everyone around me, and I had trust issues. I didn't date anyone in school nor did I spend the night with any friends or relatives. I worked hard and excelled academically. Although I loved football, I never tried out for the team out of fear that the guys would haze me in the locker room or on the field. I always believed in God, and I often went to church. I even volunteered at nursing homes and homeless shelters on weekends and during the holiday season. Therefore, I had no idea why anyone would want to hurt me.

I thought about the friendships and familial relationships that I had during my childhood. My brother and I got along well for the most part. We stayed out of each other's way. Now and then, we'd argue over the last snack cake or over whose turn it was to do the dishes. He would call me gay-bashing names, and I'd kick his ass just to show him that my sway wasn't stopping these hands from tagging that ass. He'd quickly get his mind right, and we'd go back to being cool.

My father and I didn't have the best relationship, but it wasn't all bad. I always knew he loved me, but he didn't like my lifestyle. Consequently, he said mean shit to me every chance he got. I needed him so many times, but I didn't want to risk getting my feelings hurt if I tried to talk to him about something that was bothering me. Therefore, I did a lot of journaling and kept my feelings inside. I longed for him to sit at the foot of my bed and ask me about my day. I wanted him to tell me that he still loved me no matter how I turned out. He never did. He just gave my brother and me a copy of his bank card, and he continued to run his women and his cartel. My brother would work with him sometimes. Meanwhile, I'd bury myself in books and volunteer work until it was time for me to leave his house.

I had fun times with my childhood friends. We would sometimes catch a movie or grab a bite to eat. I didn't want those nights to end. They were always nice to me and wanted me to sleep over to their houses. I always refused because I didn't want to anger my father if he knew I was the only male at a sleepover. Plus, they all had brothers and fathers in their homes. I didn't want to risk those guys either coming on to me or saying mean things in passing. So, I enjoyed the few hours of hanging out every once in a while. Then, I retreated to my bedroom where no one else existed.

After recounting those relationships, not a soul came to mind when considering who could have given Deacon Rogers access to my life. Although he knew my father, there's no way Vinny would have allowed such a thing to happen to me. Rather than staying up all night trying to figure this out, I printed the email and put it with the items I was taking to my meeting with Vivian. Then, I turned on my television and flipped channels until I finally dozed off in the wee hours of the night. I had the most important reunion of my life happening in a few short hours, and I needed to be ready for that whirlwind of emotions.

"Reunited, and it feels so good
Reunited 'cause we understood"

Peaches & Herb

6

Vivian

My meeting with Tosha was interesting, to say the least. She showed an unexpected side that made me more intrigued by her. Apparently, the empowerment exercises at the Queendom gave her a much-needed confidence booster. The Tosha I met with earlier today was nothing like the weak-willed, depressed, desperate woman that came into my office over a year ago. This time around, she seemed to be more relaxed and sure of herself. She walked with a sexy stride, and she was more vocal than before. I was so shocked by her poise that I almost allowed her to peep into my personal life. For a brief moment, I felt comfortable enough to let her into my world before the whips, chains, and revenge. I was seconds away from telling her that I was once a hurt, broken woman who longed for a love of my own. I wanted to tell her that I didn't always find pleasure in hurting men. On the contrary, I desired to be married with kids in a nice mansion. I wanted my kids to attend the best schools in the country while I ran the most successful business in the world. That's what I really wanted to share with her, but I didn't.

Instead, I quickly snapped back to reality and attempted to make her feel uncomfortable. However, her response was the complete opposite of my expectations. Like the typical Vivian, I stared her down to throw her off. Then, I invaded her space to make her fidget and submit to me. However, I found myself submitting to her. I ripped her shirt off, and she let me. I kissed her, and she let me. She even pulled me closer and controlled the kiss before leaving me hanging suddenly. That bitch controlled me, and I loved every minute of it.

As I shook Tosha's sexiness from my mind, my thoughts wandered to tomorrow's meeting with the rape victim. That reminded me that my mother never returned my call. I took a chance to try her again before writing her off for good this time. Surprisingly, she answered after the second ring.

"Hello, daughter! Sorry I haven't gotten back with you. How are you?"

"Hey, Ma! I was beginning to think you were still mad at me. I'm well for the most part. How are you? What's been up?"

"I can't complain. I've been spending time with your brother believe it or not."

"Wow… Really? Who Charlie? Surely, VJ didn't have time to pull away from his hoes – I mean, *whole*some lifestyle to spend time with Mommy."

"It was actually VJ. I thought it was strange, too. But, you know I'll take any time I can get with my babies."

"Yea, that is strange indeed. What was that all about? Is he in trouble again? Can't his rich daddy bail him out like always?"

"Don't start being so judgmental, Vivian. VJ didn't choose that lifestyle. I allowed that to happen to him. I just wanted to be done with Vincent, even if that meant leaving my boys with him," Bella said sadly.

I didn't want to upset her and risk another argument when I needed her myself. I opted to lighten the conversation a bit before getting to the nature of my call.

"So how is Charlie? Has anyone heard from him?"

"Her."

"Huh? I said how is Charl-"

Bella interrupted me. "I know what *you* said, and I said *her.*"

"What do you mean her? You're confusing me, woman!"

"Child, if you don't shut up and listen for a change. You asked about Charlie and if anyone has heard from *him.* I corrected you and said *her* because *he* or *him* is *she* or *her* now. He goes by Cheyenne," my mother said matter-of-factly.

"Well damn. When did this happen? Wait! Come again… Did you say Cheyenne?"

"Yep. Cheyenne. It's a pretty name, but you know your brother and his father hate it so much. He was just ranting and raving about it…"

"Did Charlie keep the same last name? I just think it's strange that VJ visited you and broke this news at the same time a Cheyenne reached out to me for services."

"Services? Are you still teaching these women the wrong way to deal with their grief, Vivian? What you're doing is unethical and against the Good Book!"

"Mom, look. Now is not the time for a lecture. I think Charlie… Cheyenne may be hurt. What's his last name?"

"Hurt? How do you know this? Did you know about the change? I think VJ said Jones or Johnson. Yea… Cheyenne Johnson," Bella said.

"No, I didn't know anything. But, the reason I called you is that a young lady reached out to me about being raped. I never saw her face, but her name is Cheyenne. I'm meeting with her tomorrow to discuss her therapy. I know you have a gift for working with these victims, and I know you hate my method of therapy. Her pictures broke my heart, and I knew I needed to take a more delicate approach with her. You're great at that."

"So, what makes you think this is Charlie? Did he say something that gave it away?"

"Well, no. But, this feeling in the pit of my stomach coupled with VJ's visit and revelation of Charlie's change isn't sitting well with me. Have you tried calling Charlie?"

"I've called all week to no avail. I've left several messages, and she hasn't called back yet. Now, I'm really beginning to worry. What time is your meeting tomorrow?"

"It's at 10. Don't worry yourself right now. We don't even know for a fact this is Charlie. I'll contact you as soon as the meeting is over. Meanwhile, I need you to email me some techniques for dealing with rape victims. I really need your expertise for this one. I gotta go, Ma."

"Okay, Baby Girl. I'll send you everything I have, and you can choose from there. It was great hearing your voice. Let's do lunch next week. I love you."

"It's a date. I love you, too," I said as we hung up.

I sat back in my chair, closed my eyes, and took several deep breaths to calm my spirit. A shockwave of emotions brought tears to my eyes as I thought about the pain my brother could have endured, the love/hate relationship I shared with my mother, and the fact that my period was taking me off my game. I felt like I was on the verge of losing my head as I did so many years ago when I woke up to Kyle's lifeless body lying next to me. I was reminded of the scrutiny I faced during the investigation and of the way Bella helped me fix it all. No matter how many times we bumped heads, I could always depend on my mama to help me get back on track. I will especially need her after tomorrow's meeting if my suspicions turn out to be true. I even considered blowing the dust off my journal and releasing my feelings through writing. After I calmed myself enough to fight off the tears, I packed up and went home to escape the problems of the world.

7

Bella

This day has sent me on an emotional rollercoaster. First, VJ paid me a pop-up visit and spent several hours just hanging out and talking. I thought it was unusual, but I was just glad to have at least one of my children with me for a few hours. The visit was very pleasant. I cooked and poured us some wine. Then, I kicked his butt in a few games of Gin Rummy. It felt good to spend time with him. To my surprise, he informed me that Charlie finally admitted to being gay. He's now transgender, and he has a new identity. In addition to those surprises, Vivian contacted me for help with a client. While talking to her, I informed her of her brother's new life. She immediately seemed to be in a state of panic as she asked for specific details about Charlie's new life and name. I hope she doesn't give him a hard time. She can be so judgmental and come off harsh at times.

My relationship with my kids has not been the best. As much as I wanted to be there for my boys, I didn't want to face Vincent. He's still the same controlling son of a bitch that he was when I first met him over thirty years ago. I should have fought for my boys, but I wanted to be done with that lifestyle so badly that I just took Vivian and went on with my life. She and I have always had a good relationship for the most part. She crossed the line when she tried to solicit one of my clients to join her agency. The thing is, she and I have different counseling techniques. Therefore, it was utterly disrespectful for her to try to taint my client after all the hard work we put into her recovery. It took me a while to get over being angry with Vivian. Still, I had to face the fact that I created the monster she has become.

Vivian was always a gifted, confident, outspoken child. While she played well with others, she rarely allowed anyone to become her close friend. She's always been guarded. When she was very young, she found out the truth about her father. He was an abusive drug-addict who beat me into labor with her. Then, he kidnapped me and had plans to kill me. Luckily, I woke up in enough time to grab his gun and shoot him in the head while he was puffing his crack pipe. His murder became an unsolved cold case until years later when the cops announced they had a lead.

When my sister brought the news of the lead to me, Vivian overheard the whole conversation. From that moment forward, she has had a vendetta against men. She never made friends with guys. She eventually developed friendships with females. However, I honestly feel like she sought out certain friendships to teach the women how to be in control of their lives and their men. She rarely dated any guys because she had trust issues to accompany her daddy issues. Finally, she stumbled across Kyle. He was the CFO of the counseling firm where she worked. Like most of her relationships with men, she and Kyle had a bumpy start. She thought he was cocky and arrogant. He thought she was beautiful and broken.

Eventually, he convinced her to go to happy hour with him at a nice spot off the Southern Loop. That quick non-date turned into lunch a few days later, dinner after that, and then a weekend getaway. After a while, Vivian dropped her guard and committed to dating him exclusively. She made Kyle sign an agreement that he would not intentionally hurt her. If he did, she could punish him as she saw fit as long as she didn't kill him. Because he was sure that he'd be the man to sweep her off her feet forever, Kyle signed the paperwork.

Things went well between them for a while. They took frequent baecations, went to the opera, watched Broadways shows, and experienced so many new things together. Their relationship was nothing short of perfect until a younger woman with a smaller waistline and bigger butt got hired at the firm through a temp agency. She was assigned to work on Kyle's team, which meant they worked together daily. Most times, the temp saw clients in their homes while Kyle remained in the office. On rare occasions, she assisted him with completing his reports on the clients. Quite naturally, their conversations sometimes included personal information about themselves. It turns out that the new young, small-waisted temp with the booty was single and ready to mingle.

She knew Kyle and Vivian were an item, but that didn't stop her from making advances at him. At first, he laughed them off as simple flirts. His brain reminded him that he had a beautiful woman who wasn't wrapped too tight. Still, his dick tricked him into believing he was smart enough to avoid being caught. So, he accepted the temp's advances and began to flirt back with her. He began to inbox with her on social media, he often liked pictures of her in short dresses or tight jeans, and they even texted sometimes. Now, my daughter is not a jealous woman. However, she doesn't take kindly to anyone moving in on her territory. Not to mention, she and Kyle had an agreement that she intended to enforce.

One day, she overheard Kyle and the temp giggling a little too much for her liking. So, she poked her head into the office to join in the laughter. The look on Kyle's face quickly confirmed his guilt as he quickly changed the subject back to work. Rather than cause a scene, Vivian simply closed the door and went back to her office. She sent Kyle a text message letting him know that she felt uncomfortable with his relationship with the temp. Rather than understand Vivian's feelings and respect her wishes, he told Vivian she was tripping and tried to make her feel like she was wrong for questioning him.

You see, Kyle did that a lot. Any time he was caught in the wrong, he would get all worked up and act an ass with Vivian as if she'd done something wrong. She would also ask him kindly to be mindful of the pictures he liked on social media or to watch the signals he was sending to women. He would catch a major attitude and tell her that he just won't like any pictures or talk to anyone at all since she found fault in everything he did. Vivian would kindly explain to him that she just didn't feel comfortable with his actions and she wished he would not get angry with her for expecting him to respect her. Sweet Kyle who was kind to everyone else would always speak so aggressively, rudely, and arrogantly to Vivian when she expressed herself. Vivian tried her best to get over his rudeness, but it became more difficult with each argument.

The more they argued about his utter disrespect and disregard for her feelings, the angrier she became inside. She slowly began to withdraw as she quit asking questions and confronting issues. Instead, she sat in the cut and watched Kyle. She noticed how he had so much conversation and energy for other women, but he was always so tired or in a shitty mood when it came to her. She noticed how he was a such a counselor, so vocal, and so supportive of everyone on social media, but he was always too tired to provide input on Vivian's problems. Plus, their sex life had drastically declined. Vivian believed Kyle was faithful, but she had her suspicions. Still, she didn't say a word. She was tired of fighting and arguing. She was tired of trying to make her relationship with Kyle more than it was going to be. Vivian was tired, and Kyle was in trouble.

After several years of trying to get Kyle to behave, Vivian finally snapped, and I was left to clean up her mess. I'll never forget the day I walked into her bedroom and found her sleeping next to his dead body. I had been calling them for a few days and never got an answer on either phone. At first, I thought they had gone out of town to rekindle their relationship. I was out driving one evening and decided to swing by her house just to make sure everything was okay. When I pulled up, I noticed how wet their yard was from the sprinkler system running for what seemed like days. I immediately sensed something was wrong, so I rang the doorbell twice and let myself in with the key Vivian had given me in case of an emergency.

When I entered the living room, I was hit was a horrid scent of trash, liquor, and an unidentifiable smell. In the pit of my stomach, I knew what it could have been. Still, I hoped my thoughts and intuition were mistaking me. I slowly walked down Vivian's long hallway that led to her bedroom. As I passed the hallway bathroom and guest rooms, I peeked my head into each room to make sure I wasn't missing anything. The door to her bedroom was slightly ajar, so I pushed it open without knocking. That's when I saw Kyle naked lying on his stomach in a pool of blood. Vivian was lying next to him with her arm draped across his back. She was cradling a bottle of alcohol and a picture of the two of them on their first baecation. I could tell she was alive because she was snoring like a man that had worked double shifts for two weeks straight.

After I called her name several times, she finally woke up and sat up in the bed. As she tried to focus, she took a long drink from her bottle. Then, she began to cry uncontrollably as she scolded Kyle for making her do that to him. I had never seen my daughter in such a mess. It was the most heartbreaking sight I'd ever witnessed. As my baby cried her heart out to the only man she ever truly loved, I went into her bathroom and ran a hot bath for her in her oversized jacuzzi tub. After that, I called my ex, Vincent Bourdeaux, and asked him to send his crew to Vivian's address. I didn't ask my baby girl any questions. I just cleaned up the mess she'd made of her house and her life. The only words she uttered while sitting in the tub were, "He made himself killable. I told him not to hurt me." Meanwhile, the guys took Kyle's dead body to the counseling agency and set the building ablaze. That was the end of Vivian and Kyle and the beginning of Vivian's dark side.

8

Vivian

January 15, 2018

Dear Diary,

It's been a while... I don't even know where to begin. Right now, I feel like a caged bird who can't even help my clients and family. So, you know I definitely can't help myself. Let's see... I've been having nightmares about Kyle. It's like he's haunting me from the grave. I know no evidence will lead to my arrest, but I just feel so paranoid for some reason. Bella assured me that she handled it, and I believe her. It's just that I still don't have any recollection of how he died. Bits and pieces of the events leading up to his death have come to me. I've had flashes of us enjoying a nice evening together at my place. I recall us having drinks and cooking

*together. From what I remember, we were
happy, and the night was going well.*

*I've also had flashbacks of us having sex and
holding each other in bed afterward. The
next thing I know, I woke up next to Kyle's
corpse. I remember Bella coming over with
her crew to clean up the scene. She gave me
a pill and told me it would help me forget
everything that happened. I trust her, but I
honestly regret taking the pill. I need to know
what really happened. I'm considering
investigating the issue for myself, but I don't
want to involve Bella. I don't want to offend
her and make her think that I don't trust her.
I just need answers.*

***

  As I thumbed through the contents of
Kyle's file that I kept on him, Maria buzzed
and caught me off guard.
  "Good afternoon, Vivian."
  "Sheesh! You startled me, Maria.
Good afternoon. Uh, what can I do for you?"
  "Are you okay, Boss Lady?" Maria
asked sounding overly concerned.

"Yes, I'm fine. I was just caught up in some paperwork and lost track of my surroundings. Thanks for asking. Do I have an appointment this afternoon?"

"Yes, you do. She just walked in. Miss Johnson..."

"Cheyenne! Oh, snap. I almost forgot about her. Give me about five minutes, and then send her back," I said as I quickly cleared my desk of any confidential information and checked my appearance in the oversized mirror on my wall.

Although I had seen Cheyenne before, I was nervous to find out if this was indeed my brother Charlie. I had so many questions and didn't know where to begin. I took a sip of water and a few deep breaths to relax. The lack of sleep and nightmares coupled with the multitude of emotions I've experienced lately has me feeling like a nutcase. As I paced the floor to calm my nerves, I heard a light knock on the door. I walked swiftly to the lounge area of my office before inviting Cheyenne to enter.

"Come in," I said once I was seated comfortably in the chair across from the leather sofa.

I rarely use this area to meet with clients because I don't want them to feel like they are talking to a shrink. I prefer more of a meeting feel to give them the idea that they have some say or control in their treatment. I chose to sit here this time because I wanted a more relaxed approach with Cheyenne. If we needed to kick off our shoes and chat like sisters, then that's what we would do. If she chose to move to the desk, we would do that, too. I just wanted her to be comfortable with talking to me about anything and everything. I wanted Charlie to know that I will love Cheyenne as a sister just as much as I love him as a brother.

When the door opened slowly, my heart began to beat rapidly. I tried to maintain my composure and pretend I did not know who was entering my office. Still, I felt tears trying to form, so I blinked them away and tried my best to be professional.

"Greetings, Cheyenne. It's been a while since we last saw each other. You look well considering the horrible ordeal you encountered."

"Hi, Vivian. Thanks for seeing me. I didn't know who else to contact, but I knew you would take care of me."

"No worries. Please come on over and have a seat on the sofa. Would you care for a drink? Perhaps a bottle of water, a glass of wine, or some freshly squeezed fruit juice."

"I'll take a bottle of water for now. Thanks," Cheyenne said as she moved the red fur pillows and sat in the center of the sofa.

"We weren't fully acquainted the last time I saw you. It was Tosha's show, and you were an unexpected casualty. Have you spoken to Tyrone since then?" I asked trying to break the ice a bit.

"Girl, that was a complete mess. I have not talked to that fool since then. After seeing you and his crazy ass wife in action, I knew I wanted no parts of him or his drama. I've just been busy with church, which is how I ended up here with you right now," she said as her eyes drifted to my large bay window.

"Yes, I understand. We will get to the nature of this visit in a moment. Well, I'm glad you got out of that situation. He was no good for any woman. Tell me about your family life. Do you have children or siblings? Are you close with your parents?"

"I do have siblings but no children. I have one sister and one brother. I haven't seen either of them in a while. I speak with my mother regularly, but I hate my father. And, before you ask, I do have daddy issues. I grew up different from who I am today. My father treated me terribly because of it."

"Why haven't you seen your siblings in a while?" I asked yet afraid that she'd blame me for our distance.

"Well, my brother is a lot like my father. He gave me hell growing up, so I said to hell with him as well. My father did not let my mother see my brother or me because she no longer wanted to be under his control. So, when she left, she took my sister, and we lost contact. My sister does not have the same father as my brother and me. I've seen her, but I don't think she recognizes me."

"Why wouldn't she recognize you? Has it been that long since you have seen each other?" I asked hoping she'd just come clean about her change.

Cheyenne cleared her throat before responding.

"Ahem… Like I said a moment ago, I was always different growing up, and I am a different person today from who my sister saw before she left with our mom."

Just spit it out! How are you different!?, I thought to myself.

"Would you care to explain your difference?" I asked calmly.

"I grew up feeling like I was born in the wrong body. On the outside, I was a handsome little boy, but inside I was a pretty princess. My father always knew his football player preferred pom-poms. So, he was hella mean to me. My brother often teased me about the sway in my walk. He even blackmailed me for years and threatened to tell our father my secret if I didn't do favors for him. As I stated, my mother and sister weren't allowed to see us. We spoke on the phone periodically, but they could not tell I was different by the tone of my voice. I hid it from them for years. A few years ago, I decided to do away with Charles Vincent Bourdeaux, daddy's football player, and I gladly embraced Cheyenne Imani Johnson. I plan to tell my mother soon, and I just confessed to my sister a few seconds ago," Cheyenne sighed and forced a smile through her tears.

I didn't say a word as I walked over to the sofa, grabbed my sister by the hands and pulled her to her feet before giving her a hug that I've longed to give since she entered my office. We stood in that spot for what seemed like forever, and we hugged each other as tightly as a church mother hugs a lost sinner. Neither of us spoke. We just cried hard, ugly, and loudly as we released all the pain, fear, and anger we had bottled up for years. For the first time in a long time, I was not Queen or The Fixer. I was simply a sister with a soft heart who needed the embrace of a loved one. I was a human being who was capable of crying, loving, feeling, and caring. I was Charlie's big sister who would love him as Cheyenne even more than I loved him as Charlie.

"Charlie, I'm so sorry I wasn't there for you. I never knew the pain you went through. I would never have left you to deal with that motherfucker on your own. Why didn't you call me? Why didn't you reach out to me? How did you know I was Queen? Why didn't you say anything when you first realized? And, who is this motherfucker that raped you?" I spat question after question without giving Cheyenne time to answer.

"Slow down, sis! My Lord, you act just like Mommy. First of all, love bug, I am Cheyenne, not Charlie. Charlie was a scared ass little boy who couldn't stand up for himself. Cheyenne is a bold boss bitch that takes no shit from anyone… Well except for you and Mommy. You two heffas are forces to be reckoned with," she laughed and softened the mood.

"I'm sorry, girl. This all is just too much for me. You're beautiful by the way. Now, answer my questions."

"I didn't call you because I needed time to embrace my new life. I didn't know how much judgment or ridiculing I'd receive, so I kept to myself and tried to find normalcy of my own. The moment I saw you at the Queendom, I knew it was you. Although you wore the mask, your eyes pierced my soul as they always have. I wanted to embrace you then, but your ass was on one. Plus, we had just caught Tyrone in those lies. I knew I would see you again, so I just left it alone. I was relieved to see you doing so well though.

"Deacon Rogers at my church is who raped me. I finally remembered that he is Vinny's friend from the past, and he knew who I was for a while before he started making advances at me. Like I said in my email, I want revenge. In fact, I *need* revenge. Before I forget, take a look at this email I received from an anonymous sender. I think it came from Deacon Rogers, but this person knows too much about what happened. It's just such a coincidence that I received that message a week after he raped me. I will not let this motherfucker get away with this shit. Make him pay, sis! I don't care how much this will cost me. I have the money."

I sat in silence for a moment to take in everything Cheyenne had just told me. Then, I opened the folder and viewed the pictures she printed from her email. Unless she wasn't telling me everything, this person sure did know too much about her. I tried my best to think like a therapist rather than a revengeful big sister. I knew I wanted to kill Deacon Rogers, but I didn't know how we would go about doing it. There's no telling how many other young women or gay guys he has violated and forced to keep quiet. Scum like him should not be worthy of another breath. He damn sure wasn't going to get the chance to hurt anyone else. Not only would we expose his nasty ass, but I would also get in contact with Vincent to make that motherfucker disappear. As much as I hate Vinny, I'm willing to put aside our differences to help Cheyenne. Regardless of how evil he can be, I must admit that he's cold as fuck when it comes to handling his business.

"Alright, so you know we have to involve your father in this. Right?"

"Vinny? Why? Can't you handle this on your own? I mean you've been doing this shit for years. We can torture him like we did Tyrone and like tell his wife or something. Why do we have to bring Vinny in it? I hate his ass," Cheyenne said as she crossed her legs and hugged one of the pillows.

"Listen, Chey. I hate him, too, but this shit is deeper than anything I've dealt with before. We're talking about my flesh and blood! I can't just give him a little visit to the Queendom and go on with life. He might come back for you. Hell no! He will not live to hurt you or anyone else ever again!"

"Wait… what do you mean, Viv? I can't kill anybody. And, I can't let you go to jail to save me. Maybe this was a mistake."

Cheyenne stood up and grabbed her purse as if she was about to leave.

"Have a seat," I said firmly. She quickly sat down on the edge of the seat.

"Viv, this is just too much for me. I mean maybe I led him on or something. Maybe this is all my fault. I should have just dealt with this on my own. I was caught up in my emotions when I contacted you, and I didn't even plan to reveal my identity. I didn't even consider how this would make you feel knowing he hurt your family. I'm sorry, sis. I know this is hard for you, but please let me just walk away and forget this ever happened," Cheyenne pleaded.

"Baby sis, I love you. I understand how you feel, but there's no walking away. I will move forward with or without you. I have all the information I need to make his life – or what's left of it - a living hell. I've already texted his information to Medgar, my private investigator. This ship will sail. So, are you in?"

With tears rolling down her cheeks, Cheyenne simply nodded her head. Then, she gathered her belongings, kissed me on my forehead, and headed for the door without a word.

"I'll be in contact," I said as she closed the door behind her.

9

Marissa

Things haven't been the same between Cheyenne and me since the Tyrone situation. Yeah, it's supposed to be chicks before dicks, but it seems she just doesn't want me to find love. Well, I found it this time, and she'll find out soon enough. I've been dating VJ for a few months, and things have gotten pretty serious between us. We met when he came by the shop one day looking for Cheyenne. She wasn't there at the time, and I couldn't resist flirting with his sexy ass. I didn't care if he was her man. I took her absence as an opportunity to get back at her. That shit with Tyrone damn near broke me. I fell into a deep depression for a while and had to force myself to shake back. I'm back now, baby. All the way back!

VJ is sexy, smart, ballin, and Cheyenne's brother. I didn't even know she had a family or a dick until he came into the shop that day — another lie. Years of friendship and she never found time to tell me that she was born a he. I realized then that I didn't know a thing about my so-called best friend, so I took the liberty of getting to know her brother. We hit it off immediately. One night after several drinks, I found out why VJ was looking for Cheyenne. Their father has been ill, and VJ wants to ensure that Cheyenne remains estranged and won't come looking for any insurance money if their father dies. Together we devised a plan that would benefit us both. If everything goes as planned, VJ will get the full million-dollar policy, and I would become the sole owner of Xpressions Nail Salon. All I had to do was keep up with Cheyenne's schedule, and VJ would do the rest.

At first, I felt bad about plotting with a stranger against my best friend. Then, I remembered all the secrets she kept from me and all the men she stole from me over the years. To think I couldn't even keep my man away from another man. Am I really that pathetic? I knew her body was too perfect with the perky breasts, plump ass, high cheekbones, flawless makeup, and full lips. On top of that, she is rather tall and muscular to be a woman. I actually believed her stories of being a bodybuilder and model when she was growing up. After talking to VJ, I learned that everything Cheyenne told me was a lie. Well, her lies have finally caught up with her.

VJ hired one of his dad's friends to kill Cheyenne. He paid Deacon Rogers $25,000 to do it. The day after it was supposed to happen, I gave Cheyenne time to be late for work and then I started blowing her phone up like a concerned bestie would do. I left several messages in a state of panic to pretend I was so worried about her. She didn't answer for a few days, so I threatened her answering machine that I would come over if she didn't return my calls. To my surprise, she called back, and I knew something was wrong. I immediately called VJ, and he almost lost his mind. He sent me a bunch of pictures of Cheyenne when she was Charlie and told me to email them to her with a threatening message as if it came from Deacon Rogers. So, I created an anonymous email account and followed VJ's orders.

Seeing the innocent little boy in the pictures made me wonder what my friend faced as a child. Why did Cheyenne change her identity? Why didn't she tell me? I've always loved her like a blood sister. Why didn't she trust me enough to be honest with me? My heart wanted to feel sorry for her and back out on the plan, but VJ threatened to harm my family and me if any of this got out. I was stuck at this point. Then again, Cheyenne never once asked me why I was so depressed about Tyrone. She just laughed it off and went on with her life while I faced an abortion alone. Now, it's her time to hurt while her brother and I get rich.

10

Cheyenne

My meeting with Vivian went better than expected. I can't say that I agree with the way she does things, but I finally felt the protection that I've longed for my whole life from a loved one. After years of holding on to a secret that has held me captive, I was finally able to let my hair down and be myself. I didn't have to be the person I created in Cheyenne. I didn't have to be Charlie, the macho kid for my dad and brother. I could be me. Scared, sad, alone, angry, loving, caring *me*. I could hug a loved one and let the tears flow as long as the Nile River. I could laugh genuinely, love sincerely, and cry ugly without being judged. I could talk to my sister, and she could talk to me. Initially, I thought things would be awkward between us. I thought I would be in a session with a shrink and too afraid to reveal my truth.

Somehow, it felt like Vivian already knew my truth, and she was trying to pull it out with every word she spoke. However, there's no way for her to know because I know she doesn't speak to Vinny or VJ. Plus, VJ's evil ass wouldn't even spread my business like that. He was indeed hateful towards me when we were kids, but he sometimes stood up for me if the neighborhood boys were too hard on me. I've even heard Vinny smack a few people around for saying mean things or giggling like little girls when I twisted past them. So, even though they weren't the best to live with, they did protect me sometimes.

I felt haunted by Vivian's suggestion that we kill Deacon Rogers. I mean, he has a family. How would they take his death? What if they find out I had something to do with it and I end up in jail for the rest of my life? Although I hate him, I can't allow that pain to be brought to his wife; not like that. I damn sure can't throw my life away for a piece of scum. Exposing his ass at the festival would be perfect. I'd prepare Sis. Rogers for it beforehand so she wouldn't be blindsided by the embarrassing news. I don't know how she'd take it, but at least I'd give her a heads-up. Maybe the exposure would make him pack up and leave town. Maybe Sis. Rogers would kill him herself and save me the trouble. Maybe he'd kill himself and take us both out of our misery. I really don't care how it ends, I just want him exposed and out of my life without me having to be a part of his murder if I don't have to be.

Nevertheless, it's time for me to reclaim my life and own who I am. I will no longer be a victim of rape, molestation, bullying, hatred, and reclusion. I will live my life even if that means embarrassing that dirty deacon or killing him as Vivian has suggested if it comes down to that. It's time I tell Marissa who I really am, and I need to finish dialing my mother's number. I need to let her know how much I've resented her and needed her for so many years. I need Vinny and VJ to know that they made my life a living hell, and I look forward to them both burning in hell. I need to finally live my life with no secrets, no regrets, no wishes, and no shame. It's time I let Cheyenne live the life of her dreams.

***

I let the phone ring four times before I got ready to hang up. Just as I went to end the call, my mother answered the phone.

"This is Bella. How may I help you?" her sweet voice spoke.

"Hi, Mommy. It's Charl- I mean Cheyenne. It's Cheyenne," I said nervously.

The line went silent for what seemed like an eternity. Just as I got ready to hang up, I heard my mother sniffle before speaking.

"Oh, Cheyenne. My baby. You have no idea how long I've waited for this call. How are you, baby? I'm so sorry for leaving you and not being there when you needed me," she cried. "I heard you had embraced yourself, and I'm just glad you're okay."

Through a big ass lump in my throat, I managed to say, "It's okay, Mommy. I'm okay. Well, I'm not okay, but I'll be fine. I need to see you. I've needed to see you my whole life, but now I can't take another moment of not seeing you. I need you," I cried so hard that I damn near lost my breath.

At that moment, every pain I suppressed and every emotion within me came pouring out at once. As I continued to cry, my mother began to pray for me. For the first time in my life, I heard my mother's sweet voice praying for me. The more she prayed the calmer I became. It was as if a huge weight was lifting off my shoulders. I can't remember any of the words she said, but I do know her voice and prayer were so soothing to me. They were what I needed after all the hell I had been through in my life.

"Amen. Thank you, God," she said.

I repeated, "Amen."

"Where are you, baby? What's wrong? That cry is one filled with pain. Did something happen to you? Was it Vinny? Lord forgive me, but I will fuck him up if he did anything to hurt you," she said in a not so sweet voice.

I had to look at the phone to see if that was still Mommy or did Vivian hop on the line. That sweet praying woman was replaced with feistiness and cuss words. I couldn't help but laugh out loud at how she changed on me so quickly.

"Sheesh! I see where my sister gets it from, honey! I've gone from crying and praising the Lord with you to laughing all in a matter of minutes. I have felt every single emotion this week, and I am drained. How have you been?"

"I'm sorry, and I hope you don't think I'm a heathen. I love the Lord, but I sometimes cuss – especially when it comes to my babies. I'm so glad you called me. I pray you will forgive me for not being there for you. When we meet, I'll tell you my reasons for doing things how I've done them. They had nothing to do with you or your brother and everything to do with Vinny," she explained.

"Any ill feelings I had for you vanished when I heard your voice. I wanted to confront my feelings for you, but I was comforted by you instead. Look at how God works," I said feeling at peace for the first time in a long time.

"Thank God. I have a date planned with Vivian. Let's all meet. Do you mind if I invite VJ? I'd love to have all my babies with me at the same time for once."

"That sounds like a great plan, Mommy. Just tell me when, and I'm there. I'll talk to you soon."

"Okay, baby. I love you," she said before hanging up.

I replied, "I love you, too," and ended the call.

"Life is but a dream…"

Jane Taylor

11

Vincent, Jr.

"Dad! I've fucked up!" I said before my dad could greet me on his cell phone.

"What have you done this time, son? I can't keep saving your ass every time you decide to bring the heat this way."

"I paid someone to do a job, but they didn't follow through with it. Now, there's a witness, and I'm scared they'll talk. Should I take them both out or just the one who couldn't do a simple job?" I asked frantically.

"What have I told you about ordering hits without consulting me first? Do you see what happens when you don't follow instructions? Who taught you the game?"

"You," I replied dryly.

"You?!"

"You, Sir."

"That's more like it. And, who are you supposed to report to before you even take a shit?"

"You, Sir," I said as I rolled my eyes and tried to remain cool.

"You have all the answers tonight. So, help me understand why you thought you could make a move without my consent?"

"I thought I could handle it, and I didn't want to bother you considering how you've been feeling bad lately. I didn't mean any disrespect," I said hoping he'd let up and tell me how I could fix the situation.

"I appreciate your concern, but I need to know every move you make before you even think about making it. We can't afford to have the cops snooping around. I have too much to lose and beaucoup families depending on my empire. Now, who is the original target and what's the reason for the hit?" Vinny asked in his calm voice with his Southern Louisiana accent coming through loud and clear.

"The target is a broad that's standing in the way of my money. I tried to talk to her about moving around, but she believes she's entitled to what's mine. So, I believe it's time for her to swim in the Red River," I said hoping he wouldn't ask for any details. He would not authorize the hit if he knew I was trying to kill our own flesh and blood for some insurance money on his life.

"Who is the new target, and what's the plan?"

"The new target is some old head that couldn't follow through. I haven't talked to him to find out what happened, but I do know that nigga is a liability now. This should have been an easy one, but somehow his old ass fucked up, and the broad is still around to tell the story. That's why I need your help."

"That's not enough information for me to act on at this time. It seems to me that you're the one who fucked up. You've referred to him as "some old head" as if you don't know much about him. You've called her "some broad that's standing in the way of your money" as if you barely know her. It seems like you're just pouting and ordering hits because you want some money. I'm not okay with that. I need you to get control of this situation. Find out what went wrong besides your fuck-ups. Then, get back to me with some solid information. I will not take a man's life because my bitch ass son is having a temper tantrum. I need something more solid before I make a move. Do I make myself clear?" Vinny asked without raising his voice one octave.

"Yeah, very clear," I replied knowing damn well how this was going to play out.

Vinny hung up the phone without another word. I rolled a joint to clear my mind and figure out how I was going clean up this mess I've made. If Vinny finds out I'm trying to kill Charlie, I'll be the dead one before I could even explain myself. I need to come up with a quick way to get everything back on track. At this point, I need to chill since Vinny is watching me closely. If Charlie ends up dead any time soon, he'll know I did it. As a matter of fact, I'm going to reach out to his bitch ass and act like I want to make up for lost time. I'll even call him Cheyenne just to send that heat in a different direction. But first, I need to tell Marissa there's been a change of plans.

***

"Hey, baby!" Marissa said sounding like she just hit the lottery.

"Yeah, what's up with you?"

"Nothing, just sitting around waiting for you. Is everything okay?"

"Nah, I just hung up with Vinny, and he's not trying to help me fix this shit, so I need you to finish the job for me," I said.

"What do you mean? Do you want *me* to kill Cheyenne?" she asked in a shaky tone.

"*You* didn't have a problem with me doing it, so why is it a problem for *you* to do it now? This shit was your idea any muthafuckin' way! Don't get scared now. You wanted the shop to yourself. Well, as of now, you're still part owner. So, you need to fix this shit. I can't do anything because Vinny is on my ass right now. But, no one will suspect you. Have you talked to Cheyenne since she returned your call?"

"No, I haven't. And, this was not my idea…"

"Oh, so you wanna back out on me now? Oh, what you a snitch or something? What? You in your fucking feelings or something behind that faggot?" I yelled as I took a long drag from my primo.

"No. No, that's not it. I'm not a fucking snitch. It's just that I don't…" she stammered.

"You don't what!?"

"I just don't want to hurt her okay! Look, when we first started discussing this, I didn't know you meant you would hurt or try to kill Cheyenne. I just thought… I don't know… I just thought you could just make her go away. Then, things got out of hand, and you weren't speaking rationally. I just didn't want to back out on you because I knew you would start tripping like this, and I want you to know I'm down for you."

"You fuckin' right I'm trippin'! You don't have to face Vinny! I do! And that sucka ass deacon couldn't even do his damn job! What is it with you two? Are y'all working together against me? Do I need to pay you both a visit?" I asked as I began to feel paranoid.

I finished off that primo and rolled another one to calm my nerves.

"Baby, just calm down. I can tell you've been smoking that shit again by the way you're acting. We just need to figure this out together. I just don't want to hurt her anymore. You should have heard how she sounded when we talked. Even though Rogers didn't kill her literally, I damn sure think he killed her spiritually. At this point, I don't even want the money anymore. I just can't go further with this. No one knows you and I are together. We can just get rid of

Rogers and forget any of this ever happened. What do you think about that?" she asked calmly.

I listened to her as I felt myself calming down. She had a point. I never told anyone about her because I knew I would use her all along. No one can trace Rogers back to me either. Even if Vinny figures it out, he won't do anything to me. I'm his only son since my brother decided to become a bitch. I can just get rid of that deacon, dump this dumb hoe, and wait for Vinny to die. Or, I could kill them both myself and kill her ass too since she's a witness.

"Yeah, you right. That just might work," I lied. "Let me take care of some stuff, and I'll be by there later to get some of that sloppy toppy from you."

12

Marissa

As soon as I hung up with VJ, I began to pack to my belongings to leave town for a while. I didn't like his tone on the phone. The last time he got like this, I spent a few days in hiding because of how he viciously attacked me. When he smokes that shit, he becomes a different person. He gets paranoid, aggressive, and just mean. When he's clean, he's so charming and irresistible. Right now, he's a loose cannon, and I'm afraid he's going to do something to me because his plan isn't going as expected. A part of me wants to reach out to his father because I know he's the only person who can control VJ. But, from the things I've heard about Vinny in the streets, I'm not sure if I want to cross paths with him. As crazy as VJ is, for some reason he will not buck at his father.

I also want to reach out the Cheyenne. I feel so terrible about what has happened to her. Yeah, I'm pissed that she kept that secret from me. Still, I never wanted things to turn out this way. I was mad when I agreed to take her part of the business. That damn joint VJ rolled had me feeling like I could conquer the world. It wasn't until later that he told me he had laced it with cocaine. I knew that was a different high that I was feeling. Nevertheless, I said some shit and agreed to some wild shit while I was high. By the time I decided to back out, I had realized just how crazy he is. Now, I'm stuck in some shit that's way out of my league. On top of that, I've hurt one of the closest people to me.

Don't get me wrong, I did harbor a bit of hatred towards Cheyenne out of pure jealousy. So, yeah, I was all game for VJ's plan at first. However, when I found out what all that deacon did to her, I became sick to my stomach. How could I take part in bringing pain to my best friend of ten years? All those years of jealousy turned into silly little thoughts when I considered the men I didn't like her behind. The mailman was sexy, but his ass was married, so it didn't matter that he flirted with us both. He didn't want either one of us. The FedEx guy wasn't even all that cute now that I think about it.

Yeah, he was bowlegged, but his grill looked like he had been chewing concrete or something. Let's not mention Tyrone. His ass was married, controlling, a liar, and a player who had no intention of being with either one of us. He hurt us both at the same time, so I don't know why I was mad at Cheyenne behind him. Neither of us knew he was playing us both. Now, I've let some petty bullshit get me involved in the worst possible ordeal I could imagine. I have no idea how I will fix this, but something must happen quickly.

***

After a three-hour flight, my plane landed in Las Vegas. While I waited for my luggage in baggage claim, my cell phone rang. I scrambled through my fanny pack and looked at the name on the screen. It was Cheyenne calling. My heart began to race as I contemplated sending her to voicemail. However, part of me was curious about the nature of the call. Had she found out that I was a part of the rape? Did VJ pin all this on me? What if she was with the cops trying to set me up? Then again, there's no way VJ would pin that on me without implicating himself. Either way, I would find out what she wanted.

"Hey Chey!" I answered trying to act normal.

"Hey Sis! How are you?" she asked in her usual chipper tone.

"I'm good, girl. Are you feeling better? I don't want whatever you've got."

"Trust me, you sure don't," she said sounding sad.

The pain in her voice almost brought me to tears, but I played it off and changed the subject.

"So when are you going back to the shop?"

"I'm actually heading that way in a bit. I can't stand another second of being in that apartment. I need to get my life back to normal. I will not let my situation – I mean sickness hold me down, honey," Cheyenne said. "Do you wanna do lunch today? I miss you, girl. And, we have a lot of catching up to do."

I cleared my throat before speaking, and then immediately regretted I did. After ten years of friendship, Cheyenne knows I clear my throat right before I tell a lie.

"Ahem, um, I'm not in town right now. I just landed in Vegas."

"Vegas? What's going on in Vegas? I know I said I was contagious, but you could have invited me. I need to get away, too. Unless you're out there hoeing," she laughed.

"My mama ain't raise no hoe, bih," I said playfully before lying again. "I'm actually meeting someone here."

"Oh really? Anyone I know?"

"Nah, you don't know him. He's an old friend from high school. We reunited on social media, and he flew me out here. He's working here on business for a couple of months. I finally allowed someone else in after what's his face messed over us both."

"Girl, I can't even bring myself to say his damn name either. Hell, that probably isn't even his real name anyway. Well, I won't pry. Just make sure you take care of yourself and don't fall for this dude too soon. I can't be 'round here bailing you out of jail for attempted murder," she laughed.

"Hahaha very funny. Chile, I'm just here for a change of scenery and to clear my mind. I don't even know how long I will be gone. I took care of all my clients this week and told them I'd hit them up to make an appointment in the next couple of weeks."

"Okay, sis. I won't keep you. Just let me know you're okay, and I'll take care of the shop while you're gone. I love you, chick," Cheyenne said.

"Always have," I replied feeling guilt create tears in my eyes.

"Always will," she said before hanging up.

13

Cheyenne

Marissa had a strange vibe when I talked to her on the phone. I feel like she was lying to me. She always clears her throat right before she lies. After being friends for so long, she should know that I know when she's lying. There's no telling who she's meeting in Vegas or if she's really there. I bet her desperate ass is still seeing Tyrone. If she is, that's on her. I just hope she doesn't expect me to accept his triflin' ass after all the crap he put us through. I'm not going to worry myself with it. I've got ninety-nine problems, and his lying married ass ain't one. Today, I'm feeling the best since my life was brutally interrupted. For once, I have my mother and sister in my life. After crying out all the pain, sadness, and newfound joy, I'm ready to get back to work.

When I pulled up to Xpressions Nail Salon, I sat in my car and took in the scenery. I never realized how much we need to repaint the building and upgrade our sign. The words on the door are peeling, and the bricks need to be power-washed. Like my life, my salon needs a facelift. Just as I grabbed the door handle to get out the car, my cell began to ring. *"Call from VJ,"* Siri announced.

"VJ? What could he possibly want with me?" I said to myself before answering his call.

"Cheyenne, speaking," I said dryly.

"What's up baby brother?" his rude ass said with a chuckle.

"VJ, what do you want? You don't like me, and I don't like you. So, why are you even calling me? I've had a lot to happen to me this week, and I just don't need this shit from you today. What – do – you – want?" I asked pausing between each word to let him fully understand my annoyance.

"Damn, you must have been dumped by one of those sissy muthafuckas or somethin'?" he ridiculed.

Just as I began to hang up on his disrespectful ass, he spoke again. This time, it seemed like a switch flipped because he changed his tune.

"Nah, I'm just messing witcha, Cheyenne. You know a nigga gotta give you a hard time. What's up though? You been good? Nigga was just calling to check on you. I know we don't talk much, so I thought I would reach out to ya and see if you straight. Well, I know yo' ass ain't straight," he laughed, "but to see if ya good."

I rolled my eyes and laughed a little bit. I can't stand his ass, but he always did have that charming personality like our father.

"Yes, I'm straight. Thanks for checking on me. Someone must be dying for you to be calling me and seeming to be sincerely nice to me."

"Dying? Why you say somebody dying?" he asked seeming rattled by my statement.

"It was a rhetorical statement, dude. Be cool. Oh, and before you ask, I do not have any money."

"Nigga don't need your money. You know yo big bro is a hustler like our father.

But, it would be good to break bread witcha soon."

I took the phone from my ear and stared at it for a second to see if I heard what I was thinking.

"Okay, now you're scaring me. You sure everything is okay?"

"Yeah man. We good. Just trying change nshit."

"Oh… Okay… Cool. Well, yeah, we can grab a bite this evening if you're free. Where do you want to meet?" I asked.

"Meet?" he stammered. "Oh. Uh…"

I cut him off, "See, I knew your ass hadn't changed. I guess you're still too ashamed to have dinner in public with your transgender sister huh? Bye, VJ. Call me when you grow up!"

"Bruh… Chill OUT," he exclaimed. "Nigga was just gone say you can come by my place and I was gone order us something. We can watch a game or something. You do still watch football, don't you?"

I felt embarrassed about the accusations. I'm just so used to him riding me so hard that I expected more rudeness from him.

"I'm sorry, brother. I've just had an unbelievable week, and I'm a little on edge right now. Please forgive me. Yes, I do still like to watch football – for obvious reasons," I teased.

"There you go with that gay shit, man."

"I'm just playing, dude. What time do you want to hook up?"

"Meet me at the crib around 6:30 tonight."

"Okay, that'll work," I said.

"Bet," he said before hanging up.

I suddenly remembered that I had plans with Bella and Vivian. Since VJ wanted to see me too, I figured I could call Mommy back and get her thoughts on all of us just meeting up at his place tonight. I'd call her around lunchtime to see what she thinks of that. I needed to go ahead and open the shop before customers started arriving. I got out the car and entered the shop. The place was spotless but had a musty odor. I plugged up the scented oils and turned on some jazz. Then, I proceeded to the office to grab the cash box and fill the cash register. When I opened the door, the cash box was empty on top of the desk.

"That's strange," I said to myself. "Maybe Marissa made a deposit."

I immediately logged into the bank app to check our business account. The balance didn't show any deposits since last week. I became worried, but I trust Marissa. She could have forgotten to take the money to the bank before she left town. I sent her a reminder text: *Hey Diva! I noticed the cash box is empty, but the money hasn't been deposited. Did you forget to go to the bank before "hoe-king" up with your old friend? LOL Hit me when you get this message. TTYL*

I poured myself a glass of wine and waited for the first customer of the day. As I sat idly, scenes from the attack flashed in my mind. I thought about the pain and fear that had me paralyzed as he violated me. I wondered if I should have fought more. Why did I allow him to hurt me like that? I knew I was stronger and more powerful physically. Why didn't I put up a fight? I guzzled the glass of wine and erased the thoughts. Today was a good day, and I would keep it that way. I am not a victim. I am not weak. Deacon Rogers will get his. As I poured myself another glass of wine, a candy red convertible Cadillac parked next to my car. My heart began to race as Sis. Rogers stepped out and walked toward the door. By the time she entered, I was done with second glass of wine.

"Hey Sis. Rogers!" I forced.

"Hello Cheyenne, darling. How are you?" she asked with sadness in her tone.

"I'm well. I can't complain. What brings you to my neck of the woods? May I provide a service for you today?"

"No, dear. I'm here to help you. Sit down, Cheyenne. We need to talk."

She wasted no time. My heart raced because I had a feeling where this conversation was going.

"Is everything okay?" I asked.

"Look, baby. I know what he did to you. You're not the first person he's done it to, but I want to make sure you're the last," she said as she placed her soft, wrinkled hand on my trembling knee.

Hot tears streamed down my face and trapped my words in my throat. My chest began to heave in and out as I tried to calm myself down. I managed to stand up and get a cup of water from the Music Mountain machine near the front door. Part of me wanted to push that door open and run until I couldn't run anymore. However, I knew I needed to face this demon head-on before it took over my life. I finally calmed down and found my words.

"I don't know what you're talking about, Sis. Rogers."

"Then, why are you crying and breathing like an asthmatic who just ran a marathon?"

"Oh, chile. That's just my allergies. This weather change is something else," I lied.

"Cheyenne, I know my husband raped you. I have it all on camera. I've been watching his nasty ass for a while now, and I'm sick of the way he carries on. There's a camera planted in his office and a listening device in his car. I've seen the way he's looked at you. I've seen how uncomfortable you've been. But, your kind heart and respect for my family kept you around. I've seen it all before, baby girl. And, I know your secret. I've always known. I was just waiting for you to get comfortable enough to tell me. Just know that I love you no matter what. Now, we need to figure out what we're going to do about my sick ass husband. I know your father, and I know my husband has messed with the wrong one this time. I'm coming to you for you to tell me what you want to do. So, what is it that you want to do to him?"

Before I spoke, I took in everything Sis. Rogers said. I couldn't believe my ears. At that moment, I realized that I really did not know what I wanted to do to him. When I reached out to my sister, I was angry, and the attack was fresh. After seeing Vivian, I thought I could go forward with it, but I didn't want to embarrass Sis. Rogers. Now, it's like the revenge gods have just placed her right in my presence seconds after my mind almost got the best of me. This was a sign that he had to pay.

"I want him to pay. I want revenge. I don't want to bring embarrassment or pain your way, but I need him to pay."

"Have you ever heard of the Queendom?" she asked calmly.

"Sis, what do you know about the Queendom?" I asked in astonishment.

"Let's just say that I'm a lifetime member of the Queendom. I haven't always been saved, Cheyenne. And, I'm not too saved to get revenge. Oh, and I know Queen is your sister. I've been around your family far longer than you'll ever believe."

I was taken aback by her revelation. Here I was thinking she was a holier than thou churchgoing woman who would be heartbroken to know how wicked her husband is. Now, she's telling me that she's just as street savvy as she is religious. Incredible.

"Wow… uh… I don't know what to say," I stammered.

"Say how you want him to pay, and we'll make him pay. By the way, don't trust Vincent, Jr. or Marissa. They've been seeing each other for months. My husband works for your brother. The three of them developed a plan to get rid of you so your brother could inherit the policy on your dying father, and Marissa could become the sole owner of this salon."

Again, I couldn't believe what I had just heard. *Did she say my best friend and brother were seeing each other and her husband plotted with them to get rid of me? What did get rid of me even mean? Did they plan to kill me? Is that why VJ wanted me to come to his house? Is Marissa there? Did they plan to finish the job tonight when I got there?* So many questions and scenarios clouded my head. I didn't know how to feel or who to trust. I grabbed my phone and scrolled to Vivian's name. Before I could press the call button, Sis. Rogers snatched the phone from my hand.

"What do you think you're doing?" she scolded.

"I need to call Vivian. She'll know what to do."

"Don't you think if I wanted to involve Vivian, she would be here with me? Let's not involve her right now. We'll need her a little later."

"But, she already knows what happened. She was furious to know someone would harm her own flesh and blood."

"Exactly, so do you think she will act rationally with this one? I know you don't know your sister, but she hasn't been herself lately. I think she's dealing with some demons of her own. Let's let her deal with those while we handle my husband. Deal?"

"Deal," I replied nervously. "One other thing, though. I don't think Vinny is going to care what happens to me. He's hated me my whole life. I really don't want to deal with him either."

"Baby, there's no way he can hate his own child. He might not like who you've become, but he's always loved you. Let me be frank with you, Cheyenne. You can't expect a man to readily embrace his little boy who grows up and lives his life as a woman. As much as you want your father to understand you, you must first understand him. If he didn't love you, don't you think he would have sent you back to your mom a long time ago?" she asked as she helped herself to a glass of wine.

"I guess you're right, but I still need to hear those words from him. And, what do you mean he's dying?"

"He was diagnosed with Stage IV prostate cancer almost a year ago. Somehow, it's been contained in the prostate, and it hasn't spread to the rest of the body. All VJ knows is that Vinny has Stage IV cancer. What he doesn't know is that your father is scheduled for surgery next month, and he'll be perfectly fine. So, no, he's not dying," Sis. Rogers said.

I was slightly relieved to hear that, but I still felt confused by the bombshell of information she had just dropped on me. Could I even trust her? She knows too much information to not be involved. At this point, I don't know who to trust. I'll just use her for whatever information she's willing to give. Meanwhile, I need to schedule that lunch date with my mom and sister. I do know I can trust them. I'm not sure how they'll handle the news, but I need them on my team for whatever is about to happen.

14

Bella

My heart is filled with joy. For the first time in over twenty years, I will have all my babies together with me. We're supposed to go out for lunch, but I think I want to have a little cookout with them at the house. We can sit on my deck and play some Spades while sipping Stella Rosa and listening to some old school. I assume Vivian's meeting with Cheyenne went well since Cheyenne called me after all these years. The hurt in my baby's voice almost broke me down. I didn't ask too many questions, but I could feel her pain radiating through the phone. In due time, she'll tell me who hurt her.

I really hope Vivian hasn't offered her any bad advice with all that revenge mess she loves to do. I mean, I will fuck Vinny up if he had anything to do with it, but I don't want Vivian being like that. It's time for her to find healing as well. I know damn well VJ better not have anything to do with this crap. Vivian said his showing up out the blue and Cheyenne's contact just seemed too strange. I can't say that I disagree with her. I know his evil ass probably gave my baby the blues over the years. I should have gotten my kids back from Vinny, but I knew he could provide for them better than I could. Now look what has happened. I wonder if he knows anything about this since he's so big in the streets. *I guess I'll find out shortly*, I thought as I dialed his number.

After a few rings, Vinny's sexy voice came on the line. "Bonjour mon amour."

"Hello, Vincent. We need to talk," I said trying to act as if his voice didn't still drive me wild after all these years.

"How are you, Bella? To what do I owe the pleasure of this call?"

"I'm well. Never better," I said taking a slight jab in his direction.

He laughed a little and replied, "What can I do for you?"

"I'm calling about the kids. I think something is wrong. Have you talked to Charlie or VJ lately?"

"I talked to VJ today, and I didn't like the sound of the phone call. I haven't talked to Charlie since he became Cheyenne or whatever he's calling himself these days. Why do you ask?" he replied, sounding more focused.

"What do you mean you didn't like the way he sounded?"

"I don't want to speak over the phone. Will you come to my house?"

"Your house? Vinny, you know I don't want to go there. Too many memories live there."

"Bella, please come to me. It would be great to see you. I'm not feeling well, and my doctor doesn't want me moving around too much. I'll have Chef Anton to fix us some food while we discuss the kids."

Lord, I vowed to never step foot in that mansion again. I'd finally blocked those memories from my mind, but somehow that damn Vincent can still get me to do anything for him. If I didn't know any better, I'd swear he put some of that creole voodoo on me.

"Alright, Vincent. I'll come there, but I don't want any funny business. We can discuss the kids, and I'll be on my way. Tell Anton that he knows what I like. I'll be headed there in a bit."

"Okay, mon amour. I bet you look even better than you sound," he flirted.

"Goodbye, Vincent. I'll see you soon," I said as I hung up the phone.

I quickly went to my room to freshen up before heading to Vinny's house. Since I last saw him, I had put on weight in all the right places. I'm glad I'd taken advantage of the group fitness classes that came with my gym membership. Since the weather was a perfect seventy-five degrees, I decided to slip into a short sundress to reveal to my freshly shaved legs. I put on a pair of wedge heels to make my calf muscles protrude just enough. The nice breeze was perfect to blow my dress around to reveal a bit of skin here and there. Vinny always liked when I wore gold bronzer, so I applied just enough on the right parts of my face to give myself a glow. I sprayed a couple of squirts of YSL between my breasts and thighs and on my wrists. I rubbed it from my wrists around my neck. Then, I applied a nude matte Mac lipstick to finish my look. I didn't want to appear too dolled up, but I did want to make him regret letting me go. I decided to leave my bra and thong on the bed as I grabbed my purse, cell, and sunglasses and headed to speak with the father of my children.

I dropped the top on my black BMW, tuned in to Tupac Radio, and hit Highway 1 headed to face my past. After about twenty minutes, I pulled up to the gate of Bourdeaux Estates. By past habit, I reached for the keypad to enter my code, but then I quickly snapped back to reality. Instead, I pushed the call button and waited for Vincent to buzz me through the gates. His voice came through the call box and said, "The code is still your birthday." Then, he hung up, and the gates opened slowly.

Slightly flattered but also embarrassed that I had almost slipped, I exhaled and drove down the long driveway that led to the mansion that was once my home. I drove slowly and admired the landscape. Vincent's workers had taken great care of the land over the years. I wasn't surprised, because Vinny is a class act. He's also a perfectionist and expects nothing less than the best. As I got closer to the parking area, a smile began to form on my face. The tree that we planted together was massive, but I could still see where we had carved our names in the bark. I figured he would have knocked the tree down when I left. I looked around the yard and took in the beautiful scenery. Although everything had been updated, not much had changed. Bourdeaux Estates still felt familiar to me. Before I could park my car and step out, Ernest the butler stepped outside and greeted me at my car. As I shut off the engine, he opened the door and helped me step out.

"Greetings Queen Bella. It's so nice to see you again. You look amazing as always," he said as he kissed my hand.

"Thank you, Ernest. You've always been so kind. You look well. How's the family?"

"Everyone is great. Mr. Bourdeaux is waiting for you on the terrace. Chef Anton prepared your favorite meal. I hope you enjoy."

"Thank you," I said as I followed Ernest to the terrace.

As we walked through the house, I admired the décor and paintings on the wall. I thought Vincent's taste couldn't get any better, but I was wrong. His house was immaculately decorated from floor to ceiling. When we reached the end of the hallway that led to the terrace. I stopped in my tracks. I couldn't believe my eyes as I stared at the beautiful artwork above the exit. It was a painting of Vincent, my three children, and me.

"Isn't it lovely, Ms. Bella?" Ernest asked as we stood side by side staring at the painting.

By this time, tears were streaming down my face. I couldn't speak, so I simply nodded my head.

"Mr. Bourdeaux had a young man to paint this many years ago. It has been hanging above the entrance to Bella Terrace since then," he smiled as he opened the door and escorted me to my seat. "Mr. Bourdeaux, Ms. Bella, enjoy your meal."

"Thanks, Ernest," we said in unison.

"Why the tears?" Vinny asked.

"Memories. That painting is amazing. Bella Terrace? Really?"

"Yes really. Is there a problem?"

"No, but I'm just wondering why I'm on a painting in your house, and why did you name your terrace after me?" I asked.

"Why not, Bella? You mean the world to me. Even if things didn't work out between us, that didn't change the way I'll always feel about you," he said as he took a

sip of the cognac chilling in his glass.
"Would you like a drink?"

"Sure. I'll have what you're having."

As Vinny grabbed the crystal decanter from the table and poured me a glass of cognac, I couldn't help but notice the muscle and veins that sculpted his thick arms. A light breeze blew the fragrance of Chanel Gabrielle Paris cologne through my nostrils, and I immediately became intoxicated. Damn, Vinny smelled good and looked even better. As I followed the veins up his bulky arms that were packaged underneath perfectly golden skin, I became aroused. I noticed his broad shoulders and admired his chiseled chest that peeked from behind the white linen dashiki that complimented his skin tone. My eyes scanned his chest and made their way past his thick, juicy, pink lips. Eventually, I reached his sexy hazel eyes that were a hint of gray mixed with light brown today. That's when I noticed that he'd been watching me examine his body the whole time.

"Do you like what you see?" he asked.

I laughed and replied, "In your wildest dreams old man."

"Nothing gets old but clothes, and even they make a comeback."

I laughed at his lame line and took a sip of my drink. The cognac was smooth and golden just like Vinny. It tasted so good on my tongue and went down my throat ever so slowly and sensually. It was as if the cognac made love to my mouth just as Vinny made love to me many times in the past. I thought about the countless times we made love all over this house and lawn. We couldn't get enough of each other. No matter if we had a house full of guests or if we were getting dressed for an event, if we wanted each other, we would drop everything and get busy. The way we couldn't keep our hands off each other surprises me that we didn't have more kids together. Vinny didn't believe in birth control. He always thought we'd be together forever. He often told me he wanted me to have enough kids to fill every room in this mansion and to add more rooms if needed. His charm had me hooked but not enough to continue to endure the abuse and control he had over me. While I reminisced on our past, Vinny stood up and came around to where I was sitting.

"My apologies for not properly greeting you. May I hug you, Bella?" he asked in the sweetest tone I'd ever heard.

"Sure," I said as I stood up next to his towering 6'5" stature.

He leaned down to meet my 5'6" height, and then he hugged me tightly. His grip made my lady parts throb as I took in his beautiful scent and enjoyed every second of his touch. Not only had I not seen or touched Vinny in years, but I hadn't even been with another man. The way I was feeling and the way he looked and smelled almost made me have an orgasm just from that hug.

"You look stunning, and you smell just as great," he said as he stood up and brought my body with him.

I was still in his arms as if he never wanted to let me go. I tried to keep my legs straight, but I really wanted to wrap them around his waist and ride him until we both collapsed right there on the patio. My first mind told me to act as if I wanted him to put me down, but that moment felt so great that I didn't want it to end. So, I remained dangling in his strong arms while he stared at me with those beautiful eyes that had now turned blue. They usually change colors with his emotions. Blue has always been my favorite because they turn that color when he's in love. They were that color the first time we made love and when he first looked at our boys when they were born.

"Blue huh?" I asked as he gently placed me back down.

"Always blue for you, baby," he replied as he gave me a soft peck on my lips before returning to his seat.

I stood there for a moment to regain my composure, and then I slowly sat back down in my chair and crossed my legs. I needed to squeeze my thighs together in case the juices that filled my vagina decided they wanted to drip on the pavement. Before things got out of hand and I regretted coming here, I decided to jump right into the nature of my visit.

"So, I'm here to talk about the kids. You said you didn't like your convo with VJ earlier. What do you mean?" I asked.

"He told me he ordered a hit and it didn't end well. He said it involved an older cat and a female that stood in the way of his money. He needed my advice on how to move forward, but I didn't advise him. Instead, I got onto his ass about making any moves without consulting me first. I don't even know who the targets are, nor do I know the reason for the hits. I do know that our son has lost his damn mind. I think he's back on that shit."

"What shit? Vincent, did you let my son get hooked on that same shit you've been pushing through the streets for years? How could you let this happen?"

"Bella, amour, I didn't let anything happen. You know VJ has the worst of us both. He loves the streets like me, and he's hard-headed like you. I tried my best to protect those boys, but I didn't do the best job. I guess I needed your help. It seems you did a great job with Vivian. I was wrong for keeping the boys away from you. VJ is hooked on primos and Charlie is a goddamn woman now. I fucked them up and didn't even know how to tell you or how to fix it myself," Vinny huffed as he took another sip of his drink.

"There's no time for the blame game. We need to figure out what's going on with our kids. Cheyen – I mean, Charlie. No, forget that…. Cheyenne was brutally attacked. She reached out to Vivian. Vivian called me but didn't know it was Charlie.

Around that same time, VJ visited me. I don't know all the details, but I know Cheyenne saw Vivian for counseling and then she finally called me. We're supposed to meet for lunch, and I'm inviting VJ, too. I don't know what's going on, but I hope VJ wouldn't do anything to hurt his brother," I replied.

"For VJ's sake, I hope he wouldn't either. I don't like all that sissy shit Charlie or whoever has going on, but he's still my family. I will protect family at all costs. Find out what you can and get back to me ASAP. When are you meeting the kids for lunch? Maybe I can join you guys."

"It's supposed to be today for lunch, but I'll see if they want to just come by my place for dinner tonight. You're welcome to join us."

"I like that idea. Keep me posted. I need to make some phone calls. I'll let you know what I find out."

"Okay. Let me go so I can contact the kids. I'll call you later," I said as Vinny escorted me to my car.

***

I felt uneasy as I drove away from Vinny's house. There's no way I can believe

VJ would do something like this to Cheyenne. I had no idea my babies were dealing with so much. My selfishness and fear of Vincent got in the way of me being a mother to my boys. Now, everything seems to be spiraling out of control. I need to get everyone together this evening before it's too late. Vinny and I are better together, so I'll make sure he's present as well. I touched the Bluetooth button on the touchscreen on my dash. Then, I chose Vivian's name from my saved contacts.

"Hey Ma," she answered.

"Hey, baby girl. You wouldn't believe where I'm coming from and what I just learned."

"Where and what? Is everything okay?"

"I went to see Vinny and found out that VJ is hooked on primos. Vinny says he called him earlier talking about a hit that went wrong or something like that."

"You've got to be kidding me! Do you think VJ would do something to hurt Charlie, Ma?" Vivian asked.

"Viv, I honestly don't know. I hate to admit it, but I really don't know my boys like I should. I mean, I was actually kinda uneasy when VJ visited me the other day. I was also glad to have one of my kids around. He just seemed a bit suspect to me."

"What do you mean?"

I replied, "I don't know. He just seemed off and like the visit was forced or something. He asked me quite a few questions. Even when he revealed to me that Charlie had changed, it's like he was watching me for a response. Like he was trying to see if I already knew. He even told me about Vinny being sick. I know I saw him smile when he said that. Vinny told me that VJ's hit involved an old man and a woman. Did Cheyenne ever tell you who hurt her?"

"Are you fucking serious!?" Vivian spat.

"What your mouth, Viv! What has gotten into you?"

"Ma! Cheyenne told me that a man named Deacon Rogers raped her."

"Rogers?" I couldn't believe my ears. I knew exactly who Vivian was talking about.

"Yeah. Do you know him?"

"He works for Vincent. We've known him and his wife for years. If this is the same motherfucker that raped my baby, the old Bella is about to resurface." I said.

At this moment, I didn't care about being holy and sanctified. Vengeance didn't have to be the Lord's because it would be mine this time.

"Cheyenne told me that she didn't want to hurt his family by exposing him or even killing him. She also showed me some emails that included baby pictures of her as a child. She said Dea. Rogers knew too much about her. I sent the documents over to Medgar, but I need him to get the I.P. address for the email. If this shit traces to VJ, I'm killing him myself," Vivian said angrily.

"I told Cheyenne that you and I would meet for lunch and I'd invite VJ. Vinny asked if he could come, too. Let's all meet at my house this evening around 6:30. That gives us about seven hours to gather as much information as possible. Call Medgar and get a rush on the I.P. address. I'll call everyone to schedule the dinner. I also need to contact Ava Rogers. Her husband is Cheyenne's rapist."

"Ava Rogers? Wait, she works at the Queendom," Vivian said.

"I know. She and I have had choice words about her working with my child. Vinny isn't gonna like this news. I'll speak back with you in a couple of hours. This web is becoming more tangled by the second."

15

Vivian

Bella blew my mind with the information she revealed during our call. Could VJ really stoop that low to hurt Cheyenne? What's his motive? Their daddy gave them everything they ever wanted or needed. How could he allow someone to hurt his brother? Any of Vinny's workers know not to cross him. When Ava came to work for me, she never involved her husband in the process. In fact, she never mentioned that she knew my family. Was she involved in this plot against Cheyenne? I've trusted her for a very long time. She knows what I'll do to her if she betrays me. Allowing my sibling to experience pain is the sure way to end up wearing concrete shoes in the bottom of Red River or Caddo Lake. I guess there's nothing left to do but find out directly from the source.

I dialed Ava's number, and she picked up on the first ring. "Vivian, darling. How are you?" she asked in that annoying Cruella Deville voice of hers.

"I'm not well at all. Listen, I need to ask you something. I expect complete honesty from you. If you lie or if I find out you've had any involvement, the consequences will be far greater than you've ever imagined."

"I'm listening," she replied.

I cut to the chase. "Are you aware that your husband raped my sister? Furthermore, why didn't you tell me you knew my family?"

"Yes, I'm aware. And, I didn't tell you that I knew your family because I didn't want you to refuse to help me."

"When were you going to tell me your bum ass, no good ass, bitch ass, worm toting ass, nasty ass fucking husband raped my sister? And, did you have anything to do with this shit? Is this your way of getting

back at me for something? I will fuck your
old ass up!"

In her voice of a lifelong cigarette
smoker that was still calm, she replied,
"Vivian, you know I would never do such a
thing. My husband doesn't even know that I
know it happened. So, there's no need for
you to fuck my old ass up as you so
eloquently put it. I've suspected my husband
of cheating and being inappropriate with
young girls for years. So, I planted a hidden
camera in his office. I've known your parents
since before you were born. By the time you
were old enough to remember any faces, your
mom had taken you and started a new life. I
know all about Charlie and the change. My
husband has known as long as I have. We
hadn't seen him since he was a kid, so when
he came to our church, I didn't recognize him
at first. My husband was the one who told me
who Cheyenne really was. After a while, I
started to notice how he would flirt with
Cheyenne, but she never gave in to his
advances. I've always protected her as
family. She's eaten dinner with us and spent
many holidays in our home. When I reviewed
the footage from my husband's office and
saw what he did to her, I became enraged.

What's even more disturbing is who pushed him up to do it."

"I'm listening," I replied.

"It was VJ and that damn Marissa."

"Marissa? Marissa… Mar-"

"Yes, Marissa. Cheyenne's friend."

My mouth dropped open. How in the world did VJ link up with Marissa?

"The same Marissa that visited the Queendom with Cheyenne a little while ago?"

"Yes. That's also the same Marissa that's been her business partner for years. She's also suddenly missing," Ava replied.

"So, what do you mean VJ and Marissa set this up? Why would they do that and how do they know each other?"

"VJ believes Vincent is dying. There's a million-dollar policy on his life. VJ's addiction has caused him to become greedy and careless. He wanted Cheyenne to sign over her rights to the inheritance, but she refused. Therefore, he convinced Marissa that she'd be the sole owner of the nail salon if Cheyenne disappeared," she replied.

"Vinny is dying?" I asked feeling sad.

"He has Stage IV prostate cancer, but he'll be fine. It's contained in the prostate and hasn't spread anywhere else in the body. VJ doesn't know this though. I've spoken with Cheyenne and informed her of what's going on. She immediately wanted to call you, but I didn't think you were fit for business right now."

"I'm always fit for business. It's not your place to tell my family when they can and can't speak to me. You need to know your old ass role," I spat.

"You've got one more time to call me old, and I'll go back to my old ways on your emotional ass. That's your problem. You've always talked crazy to people and scared them with your threats. It takes a real one to know that you're just a scared little girl who needed mommy and daddy's love all along."

I couldn't believe she talked to me that way. No one ever talks to me like that. Now wasn't the time to get into a brawl with Ava. I needed to get to the bottom of what was going on with VJ trying to hurt Cheyenne.

"I'm gonna let you have that for now. My family is more important than cursing you out at this moment. What's Marissa's part in all of this?"

"She's the one that has kept tabs on Cheyenne. It wasn't supposed to happen at the church, but my husband thought it was the perfect time since they were alone. It's sickening how much he enjoyed shoving his penis in and out of her rectum repeatedly. The look of satisfaction on his face showed me that he had wanted to do that for some time. I want to personally send him to meet his maker. Will you assist me with that?" she asked politely.

"That might actually be possible. My siblings and I are having dinner with our parents this evening. Maybe you and your dick-loving husband can meet us there. Mom's house is secluded. Killing two birds with one stone would be perfect. What do you say?"

"I'm in. What time?"

"Come around 8:00. Everyone should be there by then. I'll leave the door unlocked. Just enter and follow our voices," I instructed.

"Deal. I'll see you tonight," she said before hanging up.

***

"Hey, Viv. What's the word?" Bella asked.

"I called Ava when we hung up. She told me that VJ and Marissa plotted with Dea. Rogers against Cheyenne for some insurance money. Vinny has cancer and VJ expects him to die soon. He stands to inherit a million-dollar policy and the estate if Cheyenne is out the picture. Marissa is her best friend and business partner. She stands to become the full owner of the nail salon. I guess they were gonna pay Rogers to kill Cheyenne. Get this. Ava has everything on tape from the scheme to the actual attack. She's bringing her dic- her husband by your place tonight."

"Wait. What? Why?" Bella stammered.

"I figured since we'd all be together, we would go on handle it tonight."

"What do you mean by handle it?"

"Ma, whatever type of handling we'll need to do," I sighed.

"Vivian, why does this have to happen tonight? I will finally have my family together. Can't we just enjoy that moment and deal with this later?"

Bella had a point. I was also excited about seeing everyone together, but I wanted to protect Cheyenne more than anything.

My first mind told me to call Vinny and let him handle it, but I just reconciled with my mom, and I don't want to go another six months without speaking to her. I guess I'll call Ava and tell her to wait until she gets the go-ahead from me. Hopefully, I can enjoy the evening without lashing out at VJ and letting him know that we're aware of his actions. I hung up with my mom and called Ava to postpone our plan.

"Hey, Ava. There's been a change in plans. Bella wants us to hold off so she can enjoy her family tonight. Don't come over. I'll let you know when it's time. Okay?"

"She took my man, started a life with him, and now she wants me to allow her to enjoy an evening with them? She must be out of her fucking mind," she responded.

"What are you talking about, Ava?"

"Bella. That's what I'm talking about. Your mother stole Vincent from me when we worked at the strip club. He had been coming in there for several months flirting with me. We even went on a few dates together. Then, Bella started working there, and he lost interest in me. He started sitting in her section and requesting her all time. She and I used to talk about how we'd always stick together and come up together. She eventually quit stripping and started working for Vinny. After a while, he moved her into that nice ass mansion. They had the perfect little family, but he still had her turning tricks for him. I was glad when she left him and even happier to know how hard her life was after Vinny."

I held the phone and listened to this bitter ass bitch express her jealousy and disdain for my mother. I can't believe I trusted her. I thought I had researched her enough to allow her into my life and my business. I don't know this bitch at all. That's why Bella sounded a bit rattled when I mentioned her name on the phone. I wish she would have told me the truth about Ava instead of sweeping shit under the rug. I hate that secretive shit, and I especially hate how forgiving Bella is. When a motherfucker crosses me, I'm done forever. Bella, on the other hand, blames herself for shit all the time. She feels like every bad thing that happens to her is karma for the things she did when she was younger. If the God she serves will continue to punish her forever, I don't want any parts of Him.

"You evil ass bitch! I can't believe I trusted you. Did you have anything to do with what your husband did to my sister?"

"As much as I hate Bella, I would never hurt the kids. So, no. I had nothing to do with that, and I still want to move forward with our plan. I respect your family too much to allow something like this to happen. Besides, Vinny wasn't all that great to Bella. If he loved her like he said he did, he wouldn't have allowed her to keep selling her body for him. I'm glad I dodged that bullet."

I wanted to drive straight to Ava's house and put two in her head and twenty-two all through her husband's body, but I knew acting on impulse would land me in jail for the rest of my life. For Bella's sake, I opted to play it cool and let everything unfold in due time. I just needed someone on my team that I could trust to handle this the right way. That someone was Vinny. I hung up with that bitter bitch and called him to devise a plan. He answered on the first ring.

"This is Vinny."

"Hey, Vinny. It's me, Viv. How are you?"

"Vivian, what a pleasant surprise. The old man is okay. I'm not dead, so I can't complain. How have you been, baby girl?"

He's always called me that since the day we met. It always made me feel special even though I hated the pain he brought to my mother. Living with him wasn't all bad. He was always kind to me. He made sure I got anything I wanted, and he protected me at all costs. Even after my mom left him, I secretly hoped that they'd get back together. I was only six years old when VJ was born. My mother had Charlie less than a year later. However, I remember what life was like when we were there. I often wondered why Vinny never tried to help us out as we struggled to make a better life. I eventually realized how stubborn Bella can be, and I assumed she never reached out to him for help. Well, I need his help right now.

"I've been well. Just handling business as usual. That's actually why I'm calling you. We need to talk."

"Your mother came by earlier today and gave me a briefing of what's going on with the boys. I mean… with your siblings. Is that what you want to discuss?" he asked in his usual calm tone filled with the Creole accent.

"That's exactly what I want to talk about."

"Maybe I can arrive at your mother's house a little early so the three of us can talk before the others arrive. How does that sound?"

"I don't think that's a good idea. I just got some info that Mommy may not know. Even if she does know, she's not gonna handle this like I need her to handle it. She's glad to have us all together, and she won't let anything ruin that moment. That's why I need your help," I said.

"Baby girl, you know I'll give you anything in the world, but I can't go against your mother's wishes. I know I wasn't the best man to her, but her happiness always meant the most to me."

"I guess that's why you left us to struggle all those years huh?"

"I respect that. You were a child, so you didn't know everything. Who do you think gave your Aunt Shun that money to send you and your mother away when Frankie C's case resurfaced?" he asked calmly. "And, how do you think that case disappeared, and you never heard anything else about it?" he asked.

I had no words. All these years, I thought that was a secret that my mom and I shared with my aunt. I often wondered how Aunt Shun had so much money, but I never put much thought into it.

"Baby girl, just because I wasn't there physically doesn't mean I wasn't still taking care of you and your mother. Now, I may have done some messed up things over the years, but I would never allow my family to hurt. You, your mother, and your siblings are my family. I will always take care of you. Do you understand that?" he asked.

"Yeah, Vinny. I believe you, and I appreciate that. Thank you for clearing that up for me. Excuse me for getting sharp with you. It won't happen again," I replied.

"I won't hold that against you. I know you get that feistiness from Bella. That's one of the things I've loved most about her. She doesn't take any shit from anybody. She was the first woman to ever put me in my place. That's when I knew I had to have her. I just hate I never married her. I was young, cocky, arrogant, and full of myself at the time. If I had another chance to love her right, I'd do it in a heartbeat. Listen, we don't have to be at your mom's place for another couple of hours. Let's meet at the ice cream bar on Youree. You do still love ice cream don't you, baby girl?"

"Of course, old man. It tastes even better when you're paying for it," I joked.

"Anything for my second favorite girl. I'll even get you an extra scoop. See you in about thirty minutes."

"It's a date," I said as I hung up and smiled.

I've always enjoyed talking to Vinny. He's a cool dude. His charm can break through any tension or stubbornness no matter what. On the one hand, I understand why mom left him. Still, I see why she loved him so much. He's reliable and trustworthy. I'm not sure how he'll handle knowing that VJ allowed someone to hurt Cheyenne. I guess I'll find out over ice cream.

"For the love money
People will lie, Lord, they will cheat
For the love of money
People don't care who they hurt or beat
For the love of money
A woman will sell her precious body
For a small piece of paper, it carries a lot of
weight
Call it lean, mean, mean green."

The O'Jays

16

Vinny

I arrived at the ice cream bar before Vivian. So, I sat in the car and waited for her to pull up. I thought about our conversation and all the chaos that was happening in my family. Chaos. I've never liked it. Right now, my family is dealing with chaos, and I don't like it. Bella and Vivian both contacting me on the same day tells me something bad is about to happen. My punk ass son calling me and speaking erratically tells me something bad has already happened. I just need to know who's the old man that's involved in the hit he ordered. As much as I don't want to believe it, I'll assume Cheyenne is the broad that he mentioned when he called me. What I don't know is what money the old man and broad owe VJ. If any of my workers are involved in this shit, it's gonna be bad for everyone. Moving without my consent is bad for business. When business is bad, life is bad for everyone. If Vivian confirms my suspicions, VJ and anyone else involved will see me.

As I sat in my '78 Coupe Deville waiting for Vivian to arrive, I watched several families come and go. I thought about their normalcy and how easy their lives may have been. Many of the families included both parents and two to three small children. I wondered how things would have turned out between Bella and me had I given her a normal life that involved ice cream runs and walks in the park. If I had loved her and Vivian like a normal husband and father, maybe they wouldn't harbor so much hatred and pain towards men. Had I allowed Bella to raise the boys, maybe they wouldn't have such a wedge between them. However, I wasn't built like that. My father taught me how to be a kingpin when I was barely riding a bike without training wheels. My mother didn't give me the love that I needed, so I got it from the streets. That's all I knew, and that's all I could give my family.

When Vivian's Tiffany blue g-wagon pulled up, I stepped out my car and waited for her. She looked like the innocent little girl that captured my heart the day I met her.

When she smiled at me, I could see Bella's beauty radiating through her. I couldn't see my eyes, but I knew they had to be blue at this moment. I loved both of those women and knew then that I needed to have them back in my life.

"Hey, baby girl. You're just as beautiful as your mother. Good to see you," I said as I kissed her cheek and greeted her with a hug.

"You don't look so bad yourself, old man. I hope you brought enough chump change to cover this sweet tooth. You owe me several years of ice cream," she joked as I held the door for her as we entered the building.

"I cracked open the piggy bank that's been on the desk in your room waiting for you to return. I hope these two dollars can cover us both."

We both laughed as we scanned the menu. I opted for a medium cup of pecan praline drizzled in caramel. Vivian ordered a cone that was filled with chocolate brownies, vanilla ice cream, fudge, caramel, nuts, and topped with whipped cream and a cherry. We grabbed a seat in the corner so we could speak freely without taking a chance of anyone hearing our conversation. Vivian spoke first.

"Are you familiar with a woman named Ava Rogers?" she asked.

"Absolutely. I've known Ava and her husband for years. He works for me. Why do you ask?"

"Well, she works for me at the Queendom. She gave me some very disturbing information today. You're not going to like what you hear, but I need to tell you so we can handle this as you see fit."

"Go ahead," I said calmly. My heart was pounding from a mixture of anger and nervousness. I didn't like the sound of Ava working with my child without my knowledge, and I hoped Vivian wasn't about to tell me that Sammy Rogers had anything to do with VJ's bullshit.

"For starters, I didn't know you were sick. I'm sorry to hear that. Ava told me, but she said you're going to be okay."

"Yeah, the old man is paying for some things I did in the past. I accept my fate. Thanks though. What else did she tell you?"

"She told me that she recorded her husband raping a young woman in his office at the church. She also said that VJ and the woman's best friend are involved in the rape. VJ agreed to pay the man $25,000 if he could get rid of the woman," Vivian said.

"$25,000? Did she say how VJ was going to come up with kind of money?"

"Yeah, he's expecting to inherit one million dollars along with your estate once you die of cancer."

Her voice was filled with sadness as she spoke those words. Anger and pain filled my mind as I listened to her speak.

"What makes him think he'd inherit my full estate. What about his brother? Did he not think I would leave anything to Charl – Cheyenne? What about you and your mother? Would I just leave you two with nothing?" I asked.

"That's the other thing. The woman that Deacon Rogers raped was Cheyenne. He was supposed to kill her so VJ could inherit everything. The accomplice is a chick named Marissa that's been in business with Cheyenne for years. She planned to become the sole owner of their nail salon once Cheyenne was gone."

"I've suspected that VJ would do something like this for a while now. That's why I switched my paperwork and made you the executor of my estate. I knew Cheyenne and your mother would refuse to take anything from me. With you over everything, I knew you'd make sure the family got everything I left for them. VJ has gotten hooked on drugs. I never thought he would really hurt Cheyenne, but I'm not surprised by this either. As for Sammy, he will see me. I'll deal with VJ as well," I replied.

"I'm glad you said that. I told Ava we're getting together tonight at Mommy's. I told her to bring her husband by so we could confront him and VJ at the same time. Mommy doesn't want to do that because she hasn't seen us all at the same time for many years. I told Ava to chill, but she confessed her hatred for my mom, so I'm not sure if she's going to respect my wishes or not. If they're still coming, it'll be around 8:00 tonight."

After thirty-something years, Ava was still the jealous bitch she'd always been. She swears Bella stole me from her, but we never had anything. I was a regular at the strip club, and she was the only black woman there until Bella came. Just because I only tipped her didn't mean we were in a relationship. Her twisted ass made up a relationship between us and then blamed Bella for her unhappiness.

I replied, "Okay. I'll have my men posted to intercede if they show up. I don't want your mother to be disappointed, so let's keep this away from her. Don't even tell her we met today. I'll handle VJ on my own. It's time I put something on his ass like I should have done when he was a kid."

"One more thing," Vivian said as she stood up. "Thanks for taking care of Kyle for me. I don't recall everything, but I do remember you handling that for me."

"Like I told you, I'll do anything for you, baby girl," I said as I hugged her and tried to squeeze all the pain from her. "I'll see you tonight. Don't speak with anyone else until I tell you it's okay."

"Understood," she said as she got in her vehicle and pulled off.

17

Bella

It was a quarter to six, and Vivian was the first to arrive. She got her punctuality from me. We both believed that early is on time, on time is late, and late is unacceptable. When she walked in, I was putting the finishing touches on dinner. I prepared each person's favorite dish, and I even ordered a 7-Up cake from the Cake Boss bakery on Winder. The spread included loaded potatoes, four-cheese mac and cheese, pineapple and brown sugar glazed ham, sage dressing, and rotisserie chicken.

"If the bees and hummingbirds weren't flying around, I'd swear it was Thanksgiving instead of spring around here," Vivian said as she entered the kitchen and lifted lids to see what was in the pots on the stove.

"You know I had to make sure I cooked what everyone loves."

"Um hmm. You're just trying to get Vinny back," she teased.

"Back? Who's to say I hadn't kept him all along?" I joked.

"Speaking of the devil, he just pulled up. Go freshen up, and I'll finish everything."

"Good idea," I said as I rushed to my bedroom and changed into a black dress that fit me in all the right places.

By the time I came back to the kitchen, Cheyenne and VJ had also arrived. Everyone was standing around having drinks and laughing. That was a picture-perfect moment. I blinked away the tears that tried to form.

"Hey, hey, everybody!" I exclaimed. "How's it going? Y'all are having too much fun without Queen B."

"Hey, Queen. You know the party doesn't start until you walk in," Vinny said as he kissed my hand and gave me a spin. "You look dazzling as always."

"Cut all that out," VJ blurted. "Y'all are too old for all that. What's in these pots?"

"Stop hating, VJ. Y'all grab a seat while we transfer the food to the table. Time got away from me. I had to handle some business," I said as I glanced over at Vivian.

She winked her eye and began to help me place the serving dishes on the table. Cheyenne finished setting the table while VJ and Vinny chatted about a couple of donk cars Vinny purchased from the auction. I hoped the wink meant Vivian stopped Ava from bringing her husband over to ruin our evening. I didn't tell Vivian that Ava has hated me for so many years and that she'd do anything to mess up my life. If Vivian knew that, she'd probably kill Ava. Once all the food was on the table, we sat down to break bread.

"Vinny, please bless the food," I asked.

"Bow your heads. Giving honor to the Creator of the universe. It is my prayer that you bless this food for the nourishment of our bodies. Keep both our minds and our stomachs at ease. Bless the beautiful, lovely, sexy hands that prepared this divine meal for such a beautiful family. Amen," he prayed.

"Amen," we said in unison as I blushed at the compliments.

"I just want to thank you all for coming on such short notice. You have no idea how happy my heart is right now. I never thought I'd see the day that every piece of my heart would be at one table supping together. Thank you from the bottom of my heart," I said as my voice quivered.

Cheyenne replied, "Thank you, mommy. I've prayed for this moment my whole life."

We spent the evening enjoying the meal and catching up on old times. It felt good to see my family laughing and reminiscing. I hated that Vivian didn't share the same memories as her siblings, but she didn't seem to be bothered by it. She actually looked like she was at peace for a moment. It was like we all needed this time of pure love to escape everything that had been happening in our lives. VJ and Cheyenne were distant, but they did share in some of the laughs. For a moment, VJ's plot didn't exist. Watching Vinny bob his head to the music reminded me of the nights we'd dance until I collapsed in his arms. As we fellowshipped with our kids, our song fell in the Pandora mix.

"Usually when two people are together for a long time, things seem to

change. It's been said that nothing good lasts forever, but this love gets better every day. We get all excited inside every time that we get alone. He still got love in his eyes, and I still got love in my soul."

As Tamia's sultry voice bellowed through the speakers, Vincent walked over to me and pulled me to my feet. Then, he grabbed my hands and led me to the middle of the floor. He pulled me close to him, and we slow danced through that song and the few that followed. While we dipped and swayed, I felt like I was floating. I forgot the kids were there as Vinny and I drifted off into a place where only the two of us existed. I heard the faint sounds of laughter in the background, but that didn't stop us from enjoying that moment together. Suddenly, I heard a window shatter, and Cheyenne screamed.

"Everybody get down!" Vincent yelled as he pulled his strap and ran towards the window.

"What the hell is going on?" I asked as I grabbed my 9mm from the mantle and followed Vinny.

Vivian was right behind me as Cheyenne crawled on the floor like a soldier in combat. I didn't know where VJ was.

"Turn off the lights and keep quiet," Vinny instructed.

Cheyenne stretched her arm up the wall in an attempt to reach the light switch from the floor. However, she wasn't successful.

"Your faggot ass is gonna have to stand up and be a man," VJ scolded as he stepped over Cheyenne and flipped off the light switch.

I laughed a little inside as I peered out the window to see what was going on outside. It looked like secret servicemen were all over my lawn. Several men dressed in black surrounded my house. About four others were carrying two people towards the house. They were tied up with pillowcases over their heads. I had no idea what was going on, but we would soon find out. Vinny opened the front door and let the men bring the two people inside. I immediately recognized each of the guys dressed in black. They worked for Vinny.

"VJ, grab a couple chairs and place them in the middle of the living room floor.

Cheyenne, close all the curtains," Vinny ordered.

They quickly followed his instructions while Vivian and I stood there and waited for the covers to be removed from the two mystery people. We both suspected who they could be, but we needed to see for ourselves. Once the two were secured in the chairs, Vinny snatched the coverings from their heads, and VJ flipped on the lights. Sure enough, it was Ava and Sammy Rogers in the flesh.

"I thought I told you to wait," I whispered to Vivian.

"I told Ava not to come, but I had a feeling she would. That's why I reached out to Vinny."

"You did what? When was this?" I asked.

"There's no time to discuss this right now. I'll fill you in later," she replied.

Vinny stood in front of the couple with his gun pointed at them. VJ stood nervously next to him. His gun was also pointed at them, but his hands were shaking.

"Would anyone like to tell me how our lovely evening got to this point?" Vinny asked without taking his eyes off the couple.

No one responded. Cheyenne sat in the corner crying and shaking terribly. Vivian ran over to comfort her. I took my position next to Vinny and pointed my weapon at Ava.

"Long time no see," I said.

"Likewise," Ava replied.

"Sammy," I said.

He didn't reply, so Vinny smacked him in the nose with the gun.

"Bella spoke to you. Acknowledge her, please," Vinny said.

"Good evening, Bella," Sammy said as blood poured down his nose and entered his mouth. He turned his head and spit on the floor next to him. "What's up, VJ? It's good to see you again."

VJ's eyes quickly darted to Vinny and then back to Dea. Rogers, but he never said a word. His hand began to shake more. It looked like he was about to break at any moment.

"VJ, is there anything you need to tell me?" Vinny asked.

"N- Nah. Nah, I'm good," he lied.

"Come on, baby. You stutter when you're lying. Let me ask you again. Do you need to share anything with me?"

"Nah pops. I ain't got nothing to say."

"Ava, did you bring the flash drive?" Vivian asked.

"Yes, it's in my back pocket."

I slapped Ava to the floor. She landed on her side, so I rolled her to her stomach and removed the flash drive from her back pocket.

"VJ, please do the honors," I said.

He slowly crossed in front of Vinny's gun that was still pointed at Sammy. He grabbed the drive from me, and inserted it into the smart T.V. Everyone faced the screen and waited for the video to start. Vivian and Cheyenne helped Ava to her seat. The video started at the beginning of the night Sammy assaulted my child. The look on VJ's and Sammy's faces had guilt written all over them. As the video played, Cheyenne began to vomit. Ava began to cry. Vivian slowly untied her hands and feet. Vinny grabbed VJ by the neck and pressed him against the wall as VJ's gun fell to the floor. Ava leaned down and picked it up and then pointed it at Sammy's head.

"You sick son of a bitch!" Ava shouted. "How could you do something like this? I've dealt with your cheating ass ways for years. I thought you'd eventually grow old and tired of stepping out on me. I guess the women weren't enough for you. You had to switch to the other side and sample men, too, I see. Well, I'm gonna see to it that you don't hurt another person. Count your seconds, motherfucker!"

Suddenly, Cheyenne ran in the direction of Ava and Sammy. She dove on top of Sammy and began to punch him repeatedly. Ava fell to the floor but got up quickly and aimed her gun at the two as they tussled. VJ kneed Vinny in the balls and tried to run for the front door, but one of the workers caught him with a right and knocked him unconscious. As Vinny struggled to catch his breath, Ava pulled the trigger and both Cheyenne and Sammy instantly stopped moving. A puddle of blood formed under their bodies. There was so much blood that I couldn't tell who was shot. I ran over and grabbed Cheyenne into my arms. She was covered in blood.

"I'm okay, Mommy," she said. "It wasn't me."

I sighed, "Thank God. I finally got you back. I would have lost my mind if you'd have left me so quickly."

We turned to Ava as she stood over her husband's bleeding body. He was unconscious, but he was still breathing. The bullet went through his shoulder. Lucky for him, she was a bad shot. Otherwise, he would be meeting his maker right now.

"Are you okay, honey?" I asked as I sat on the sofa next to Vinny.

"Yeah, I'm good. But, this ain't over. Vivian, let's take a trip to the Queendom," he said.

"I'm ready whenever you are."

"Paul and Peanut, load these two in the back of the suburban."

The guys followed Vinny's orders, and we all loaded up and headed to the Queendom. It was time for VJ and Sammy to pay for what they did to my baby.

18

The Queendom

We arrived at the Queendom and immediately transported VJ and Sammy to the chamber. The guys put each of them in separate rooms and dropped the temperature below freezing. Then, they stripped them butt naked and left them alone on the cold concrete floors. Vivian cleared all the guests from the chamber and instructed one of her workers to keep this area free until further notice. After that, we gathered in the hallway to discuss what we planned to do with the two assailants. Vinny spoke first.

"Vivian, this is your house and your rules. Tell me what you want to do, and we will oblige," he spoke slowly.

Usually, when he spoke in this tone, he was furious and ready to kill someone.

"I think Cheyenne should call the shots on this one. She's the victim," she replied.

"What about me? I'm also in pain," Ava added.

"Look, bitch. This is not about you right now. Your sick ass husband hurt my baby. It's her turn to get revenge. You had your chance, and you shot the muthafucka in the shoulder. Let some real gangstas handle this shit," Bella said.

Usually, Ava was quick to snap back. This time, she simply turned and walked down the hall to cool off. As bad as she wanted to be, she knew Bella would mop the floors with her if she stepped out of line.

Vinny said, "You're right, baby girl. Cheyenne, what do you want to do?"

Cheyenne walked to the window of the room VJ occupied and stared at him. He sat in the middle of the floor crying like a baby. He seemed remorseful. Then, she walked over to Sammy's window and stared at him. He was walking around laughing as blood poured from his nose, mouth, and shoulder. He was shouting, and spit flew from his mouth with every word. No one could hear him through the sound-proof windows. However, nothing about him said he felt bad for what he did to her.

"Kill him," a low voice said.

It was Ava. She had rejoined the group as they watched Sammy act a fool in the room.

"I want his ass dead. I know this isn't about me, but that's what I want. Look at him. He doesn't care that he hurt you, Cheyenne. Hell, he doesn't care that he hurt me. That animal has betrayed each of us. He's betrayed our marriage. He betrayed your trust, Vincent and Bella. And, Vivian, he's hurt the people you love the most. I think we can all agree that he doesn't deserve to live another day."

Everyone stood quietly as Ava spoke. She made valid points.

"I agree with Ava," Cheyenne said. "I've witnessed some of the things she's said. Moreover, what he did to me made me want to take my own life. I almost robbed myself of the beautiful evening we shared tonight because of the pain that monster inflicted on me. Kill that motherfucker, Dad. I want him gone!" she cried. "Just don't hurt my brother."

Vivian and Bella stood next to Vinny ready to do whatever he wanted to do. Deep inside, they felt sorry for VJ and couldn't bear the thought of having to kill him. Still, his betrayal of the family was a serious matter that could not be taken lightly.

"What do you want me to do with VJ?" Vinny asked.

"Let him live, Dad. It's not his fault that he's that way. It's yours and yours," she said as she pointed at Vinny and Bella. "We needed both of you, and neither of you was there for us. I don't blame VJ for being angry. I know all about what he and Marissa planned to do to me. Ava told me shortly after I visited Vivian. Now, I'm not gonna stand here and pretend that it didn't shatter my heart to know that my brother would do something like that to me. However, I know he wasn't acting in his right mind, and I forgive him. I don't trust him, but I forgive him for hurting me. I also forgive both of you for abandoning us."

Bella began to cry as she walked over and hugged Cheyenne. Vivian joined the hug, and the three of them shed years of bottled up tears. They cried for all the times they needed each other. They cried for all the times they resented each other. They even cried for the good times they would have in the future. Vinny's eyes were a deep brown as he looked back and forth between VJ and Sammy. His eyes turned this color when he was full of rage, and nothing enraged him more than seeing the people he loves in pain. He slowly walked over to VJ's window and stared at him. VJ stood to his feet and shivered as he walked closer to the window and stood face to face with his father. As Vinny stared at VJ, his brown eyes began to soften as they turned gray and light brown. VJ must have noticed the change because he sighed deeply and fell to his knees crying.

Vinny turned and walked over to Sammy's window. Sammy was still laughing and shouting obscenities at the group. Ava stared at him with so much hatred in her eyes. Vinny's eyes were now the deep brown of rage again. He slowly walked to the door of Sammy's room and twisted the knob to enter. Sammy stopped yelling and stood in the middle of the room smiling. Everyone joined Ava at the window and watched as Vinny cocked his gun and stood a foot away from Sammy.

"Bring VJ to me," Vinny told his workers.

They quickly opened VJ's door and escorted him to Sammy's room. No one uttered a word as they watched to see how Vinny would avenge Cheyenne's pain.

"Is this who you plotted with against my child?" Vinny asked VJ.

"Yes sir," he said with his eyes to a floor like a little boy that had broken the rules.

"Look at me when I'm talking to you boy," Vinny said without raising his voice.

VJ quickly lifted his head and looked his father in the eyes. His hands hid his penis that had been exposed and shriveled up from the cold temperature.

"Stand next to me," Vinny ordered.

VJ quickly took his position next to his father. Vinny handed him the gun.

"Press the gun to his head and pull the trigger."

"I can't do that, pop. You know I hate blood, man."

Vinny punched VJ in the mouth and knocked one of his gold teeth to the floor.

"Don't tell me what you can't do. You could allow this prick to hurt your flesh and blood, but you can't pop this motherfucker like I ordered you to do? It's either you or him. You decide."

VJ gripped the gun, took a deep breath, and walked closer to Sammy who was no longer smiling and talking shit like he had been the whole time. He was shivering and staring at Ava who never took her eyes off him. Sammy didn't speak, but he mouthed, "I'm sorry." Ava began to cry.

"I said pop him!" Vinny yelled.

Just as VJ was going to pull the trigger, Ava stopped him.

"Wait! Let me do it," she said.

"You think I'm gonna trust you with a loaded gun. Nah, hoe. I don't think so," VJ said as he shot Sammy between his eyes.

His lifeless body landed on the cold floor, and blood quickly filled the area.

Vinny grabbed the gun from VJ and pointed it at him.

"Pops? What you doing, man? You gone kill your own son?" VJ stammered.

"Weren't you going to kill Cheyenne and spend my insurance money when I died?"

"Uh nah, man. It wasn't nothing like that."

"That's not what Ava told me," Cheyenne said. "She told me all about how you were paying her husband to kill me. And how you used my best friend to plot against me. How could you do me like that, bro? You had daddy's love. I had nothing. Wasn't that enough for you? Why would you hurt me like this? We're family, VJ," Cheyenne shouted.

"Look, man. That shit be having me fucked up in the head, man. I was never going to hurt you. I could have taken you out myself if I really wanted you gone. Sammy was on that gay shit, and he did that shit out of pleasure. I had been told him I changed my mind about doing the shit."

"That should never have been a thought," Bella said as she walked towards VJ with her gun pointed at him.

"Ma, put the gun down," Vivian said.

Vinny had one gun pointed at VJ while Bella stood with hers pointed in the same direction. Tears flowed down her cheeks as she cocked the gun and pulled the trigger. The bullet went straight through Ava's head and grazed VJ's ear. Ava fell to the ground and landed on top of her husband. VJ grabbed his ear and couldn't believe he was alive.

"Ma! What the fuck?!" he yelled. "You just tried to kill your son."

"If I wanted to kill you, you'd be on top of this pile of bodies right now. I'm not like you; I'd never hurt my family. Your ear will heal in no time. Meanwhile, Cheyenne's hurt will forever be broken. If you don't get yourself cleaned up, I promise I won't miss the next time."

Vinny lowered his gun and ordered his men to clean up the mess. Then, he removed his coat and gave it to VJ so he could cover his body. Vivian and Cheyenne stood in the hallway as the rest of the family exited the room and joined them.

"This isn't the end of this, VJ," Vinny said. "I'll get you in rehab like your mother suggested. Then, we'll discuss how you'll fix this. Do I make myself clear?"

"Yes sir," VJ said sounding like a little boy being scolded.

Vinny walked over to Bella and kissed her. "I'm sorry I ruined our family. Allow me to make this right."

"I'll consider it if you promise to keep dancing with me," she flirted.

"Laissez les bons temps rouler,"
Vinny said as he grabbed Bella's hand and
led the family out the queendom.

Epilogue

"Hey, girl. When do you plan to come back to the shop? I know you can't still be in Vegas," Cheyenne said.

"I'm actually pulling up now. I was going to surprise you. I'll see you when I get in there," Marissa said as she parked and walked into the nail salon.

Cheyenne stood and greeted Marissa with a tight hug.

"Before we go any further, I need to come clean about something," Marissa said.

"Come clean about what? You been fucking with Tyrone's dusty ass?"

"Nah, it's way worse than that. First, here's the money from the cash box. I never made it to the bank. In all honesty, I never intended to go to the bank."

"What did you intend to do?" Cheyenne asked, playing dumb.

"Disappear… with… your brother," Marissa confessed.

"My brother? VJ?"

"Yeah, VJ."

"So, he was going to Vegas with you? What? Y'all planned to elope or something?"

"Nah, I actually went to Vegas because I was afraid of him."

"You're confusing me," Cheyenne said. "Were you running away to Vegas with him or were you running to Vegas to get away from him?"

Marissa replied, "I was running to get away from him after he plotted to kill you. Your father is dying and VJ wanted you out the picture so that he could get the money from the insurance policy."

"Okay, and what did you have to do with all this?"

"I was supposed to keep tabs on you so that he could have someone to kill you, but I couldn't go through with it. When he realized that I was backing out on the plan, he started acting all crazy with me."

"So, at first you were willing to work with someone to kill me?" Cheyenne asked as she stepped closer and closer to Marissa with each word.

"Yes. I mean no. No, I was never okay with it. He had me smoking that shit with him, and I must have agreed to work with him or something. I just know when I sobered up, he kept talking about it, and I was too afraid to back out of it. I don't even really remember agreeing to the shit. I just know I needed to leave town for a while so he wouldn't make me do anything to you."

By the time Marissa finished explaining herself, Cheyenne had a knife pressed to her throat.

"You're a lying ass bitch. I've known about this shit all along. I was just wondering when you'd find the time to tell me. Before I kill you, let me let you in on a little secret. I have always been the sole owner of Xpressions Nail Salon. You remember when you were too sick to meet with the attorneys, and you trusted me to sign everything? Well, I removed your name from all the paperwork and put the business in my name only. So, even if you had killed me, you wouldn't have gotten a goddamn dime of my money. Thanks for the confession though," Cheyenne said as she slit Marissa's throat and watched her bleed until she took her last breath.

Then she picked up the phone and pressed the speed dial.

"Hey, sis. It's handled."

A READING GROUP GUIDE

Thy Queendom Come

Written by
Viv Love

About this Guide

The following questions are intended
to enhance your group's reading and
discussion of Viv Love's

Thy Queendom Come

DISCUSSION QUESTIONS

1. If you've read *Daddy Issues*, what do you think of Vivian in this book compared to how she was in *Daddy Issues*?
2. Were you shocked to find out Cheyenne's identity?
3. What do you think of Tosha's behavior at Vivian's office?
4. What do you think of Vinny?
5. Do you think Vivian and Bella have anything in common?
6. What do you think of Bella?
7. What do you think will happen between Bella and Vinny?
8. Were you surprised by Bella's actions at the Queendom?
9. Do you think VJ will change?
10. Were you shocked by Cheyenne's actions at the end of the story?

More books by this author:

Daddy Issues

Available in paperback and e-book

Order at
www.valpughlove.com
or
amazon.com/author/valpughlove

www.ingramcontent.com/pod-product-compliance
Lightning Source LLC
La Vergne TN
LVHW051057080426
835508LV00019B/1924